PUZZLE NINJA

PUZZLE

パズル忍者

NINJA

PIT YOUR WITS AGAINST THE
JAPANESE PUZZLE MASTERS

ALEX BELLOS

CHRONICLE BOOKS

SAN FRANCISCO

First published in Great Britain in 2017
by Guardian Books and Faber & Faber Ltd

First published in the United States of America in 2018
by Chronicle Books LLC.

Library of Congress Cataloging-in-Publication Data available.
ISBN 978-1-4521-7105-0

Manufactured in China.

Large illustrations throughout by Leremy/Shutterstock.com
Small ninja icons throughout by Pensiri/Shutterstock.com
Design by Anna Green at siulendesign
Cover design by Anna Green and Neil Egan

Chronicle Books LLC
680 Second Street
San Francisco, CA 94107

www.chroniclebooks.com

10 9 8 7 6 5 4 3 2 1

TO BARNABY

Contents

INTRODUCTION

I'm in a bar in downtown Tokyo with a man known as Edamame (or 'Soyabean Pod').

I ask, are you a puzzle ninja?

Edamame is silent as he considers my question. 'Ninjas are associated with nimbleness and agility,' he says.

'He is very nimble,' interjects his friend nyoroppyi. 'And ninjas have lots of tricks. He fits that description perfectly!'

Edamame is – surely – a puzzle ninja. Maybe *the* puzzle ninja. Aged 24, he is a former winner of the World Puzzle Championship, and together with nyoroppyi and a few others he runs a fanzine which is a vehicle for some of the most fiendish logic puzzles ever to have made it into print.

I have come to Tokyo to meet Edamame and his entourage of enigmatologists because Japan is the global nexus of one of the most addictive products known to man, the pencil-and-paper logic puzzle. These intellectual stimulants have colonized whole sections of the world's newspapers, magazine racks and bookstores. Sudoku, the best-known type, is perhaps Japan's most successful cultural export of recent years.

But there are hundreds more: Kakuro, KenKen, O'Ekaki, Hashiwokakero, Shakashaka, Shikaku, Kurodoko, to mention only the ones with two k's in their name. Most are unknown beyond Japan. These puzzles, like Sudoku, are all set in grids, are language-independent and have very simple rules.

For me, Sudoku is now a rather tired standard. Its solving strategies are repetitive and the buzz I get from solving them has diminished over time. But it was the first Japanese puzzle to hook me, a necessary gateway drug to the Far Eastern pharmacy of magical brain food that I subsequently discovered, and which this book presents and explores. These puzzles inspire and intoxicate me much more than Sudoku ever did.

In Japan, the grid logic puzzle has become an art form. The puzzles reflect the country's fondness for miniaturism, minimalism, refinement and craftsmanship, and are a natural fit in a culture at ease with following clearly defined rules. Indeed, Japan sustains a vibrant cottage industry of puzzle creators, artisans who write all their puzzles by hand, rather than by computer as is generally done in the rest of the world. Many of these creators, like Edamame and nyoroppyi, use pen names, following the Japanese tradition also used by haiku poets and artists.

Japan's puzzle masters ensure their creations look beautiful, usually arranging the initial elements in the grid with a sense of pattern and symmetry. They also aim to provide maximum intellectual entertainment. One of the pleasures of solving a Japanese puzzle is that you can feel the hand of the author, in the way the puzzle leads you down certain paths, or reveals aesthetically pleasing patterns.

I love solving Japanese puzzles because the road to the solution is so structured: you start by looking for the first step, which will lead you to the second step, and so on, until the puzzle is complete. The first step – say, the shading of a cell, the scribbling of a number or the drawing of a section of line – is often easy to find, a 'free' move, planted to lure you in. Once you've started, that's it. You are in the puzzle's grip, committed to finishing it.

As you progress towards the solution, each new step brings excitement – a rush of serotonin – and a scramble to see what doors it has unlocked. Japanese logic puzzles drip-feed you micro-satisfactions, which is, of course, what makes them so addictive; I'd say they are the most fun you can have with a pencil and paper. Even when you hit a block, you know that there is a way through. And when you find it, wow! It is supremely uplifting to break through the wall using logical deduction alone. It makes you feel like you can overcome any other problem in the world.

Japanese puzzles are also remarkable in their variety, despite superficially looking similar, and in how their simple rules lead to sophisticated problems. When I am solving them, I lose sense of time. I am transported into the world of the puzzle in front of me. The journey to complete the grid – the many small steps, the inevitable wrong turns and the seemingly insurmountable obstacles – is always an epic adventure, and a metaphor for life.

Between the seventeenth and nineteenth centuries, when Japan isolated itself economically and culturally from the rest of the world, the country developed a unique approach to mathematics and puzzles.

Japan's oldest puzzle book, the *Wakoku Chie-Kurabe*, from 1727, contains problems not found anywhere else in the mathematical literature of the time, such as how do you fold a sheet of paper, make a single cut, and create a triple diamond shape? (In the rest of the world, puzzle books tended to draw on a shared heritage of problems, many of which were based on arithmetic.) In 1742, a Japanese publisher printed a small volume about a puzzle in which you must rearrange seven pieces to make other shapes. It is the oldest book about a physical puzzle known to exist.

At around that time Japanese mathematicians began to hang tablets containing mathematical imagery at shrines. These tablets, called *sangaku*, displayed beautiful painted geometric figures and a small amount of text, which were usually the final answer to a problem. *Sangaku* allowed their creators to share puzzles with other people, and also to throw down the gauntlet for solutions. The Japanese taste for mathematical challenges is also evident in the tradition of puzzle boxes, hand-made wooden boxes made as souvenirs that can only be opened using the correct sequence of presses, pulls and twists. Puzzle boxes are similar to the logic grid puzzle in that they are individually made by craftsmen, and they both require a step-by-step approach to solving.

Maki Kaji was well aware of Japan's puzzle traditions when in 1980 he founded the magazine *Puzzle Communication Nikoli*. Two of the first puzzles he introduced were based on numbers. He had spotted them in American magazines, but rebranded them with Japanese names. Number Place became Sudoku, and Cross Sums became Kakuro.

When *Nikoli* invited readers to come up with ideas for its own puzzles, the suggestions were stongly influenced by the grid-based style of Sudoku and Kakuro. *Nikoli* soon became a publication mostly written by its readers, who were sending in hundreds of ideas for new types of puzzles, and producing thousands of examples of them for publication.

Nikoli became – and still is – a unique laboratory for the creation of new puzzles. Puzzles are submitted, showcased, criticized, improved, refined, named, copied, and if, at the end of this process, after a couple of years, readers are still producing examples and enjoying solving these examples, the puzzle will join the ranks of *Nikoli* signature puzzles, which so far contains about thirty different types. I've chosen my ten favorites in this book, with ten examples each. Currently *Nikoli* has about 500 active puzzle creators, ranging from ten-year-old children to people over ninety.

Sudoku, the puzzle formerly known as Number Place, returned to the West thanks to a New Zealand tourist, Wayne Gould, who picked up a copy of *Nikoli* when on holiday in Tokyo in the late nineties. In 2004, he showed the puzzle to the London *Times*, which printed its first Sudoku almost immediately. With the ferocity of a viral pandemic, the puzzle spread to newspapers all over the world. The craze for Sudoku – at one point in 2005 six of the top fifty bestselling books in the US were Sudoku titles – created a demand for other Japanese puzzles.

Newspapers began to publish Kakuro, as well as many twists on Sudoku, such as Killer Sudoku, or variations on different-sized grids. A puzzle page without at least one Japanese puzzle is now not worth the paper it's printed on. The vogue for Japanese puzzles has tapped into a wider fad for brain training, and also the revived interest in activities that require pencil and paper, like coloring in, as a reaction against the digitalization of life. Another reason that helps explain the popularity of Japanese logic puzzles in the West is their exotic names. Sudoku sounds so much more ... *enticing* ... than Number Place. The name encapsulates our sense of awe towards the wise and mysterious East. Japan is a society whose language and customs are very different to our own; it feels appropriate for puzzles to come from a place we find so puzzling.

Nikoli may have consolidated the genre of the Japanese logic puzzle, but it is not the only source. Indeed, one of the reasons

Nikoli innovated so much in its early days was its rivalry with *Puzzler*, a magazine that also encouraged its readers to send in ideas. *Puzzler* published harder puzzles than *Nikoli*, which made it less popular, and it folded in 2000. Yet it was a hothouse for a generation of puzzle makers, such as Tetsuya Nishio and Naoki Inaba, both of whose work I also include in these pages. Nishio is the father of the scene and Inaba, the world's most prolific single creator of logic puzzles, is his greatest protégé.

Which brings us back to Edamame. He is part of the latest wave of Japanese puzzle masters. Their fanzine *Toketa?*, featured in Chapter 5, is taking the Japanese logic puzzle scene in entertaining new directions.

Here are some tips on how to get the most from this book:

- Get yourself a good pencil. Obviously.
- Get yourself a good eraser. Even puzzle ninjas rub out a lot.
- Always start with the easiest examples. You will need time to familiarize yourself with each puzzle's rules, and to figure out the basic strategies that will be required in the harder examples. But also, the simple puzzles have a different 'taste'. Savor it.
- When you are stumped, sometimes the best thing to do is to stop thinking about the puzzle and do something else. When you return to the problem later, the next step is quite often staring you in the face. I have lost count of the number of times this has happened to me, and it fuels the addiction, since whenever you are away from the unsolved puzzle you are itching to get back to it.

All the puzzles in this book have been designed so that each step can be deduced logically from previous steps without guesswork.

There is only one correct solution for the completed grid. No technical mathematics is required to solve them. The difficulty level is denoted by the number of mini-ninjas: 🥷 (easy), 🥷🥷 (medium), 🥷🥷🥷 (hard) and 🥷🥷🥷🥷 (very hard).

Laura Taalman, a professor of mathematics at James Madison University in the US, teaches Japanese logic puzzles to her humanities students in order to give them first-hand experience of what it is like to be a mathematician. The strategies you work out in the simple examples are analogous to theorems. Once you have nailed the strategy, you can re-use it, like a theorem, without proving it again.

I agree with Laura; these puzzles give the lay person an insight into mathematical thinking. But I also love Japanese logic puzzles because they are universal. They are a rare cultural artifact accessible to all humans, irrespective of nationality or age or gender.

All you need is a brain.

And a pencil.

Oh ... and that eraser.

THE
PUZZLE
CAVALRY

In 1980, Maki Kaji's new puzzle magazine was going to press but he still didn't have a name for it. A horse-racing enthusiast, he chose the name of something close to his heart: Nikoli, the favorite in that year's Epsom Derby. The nag didn't win. The mag, however, was a unique success, becoming Japan's most longstanding and consistently innovative puzzle magazine.

Kaji is famously playful and hedonistic. Puzzles to him are one of life's pleasures, which he enjoys as much as he does drinking, smoking and betting on the gee-gees. When we meet for a sake-fueled dinner by the *Nikoli* office he is excited to tell me about his latest madcap project, MegaCross, the world's largest ever crossword. (Japanese does not have an alphabet, so its crosswords are based on syllables, not letters.) Four members of his staff took four years to write its 59,365 across clues and 59,381 down clues, each set in its own thick volume. Kaji recently had to hire a sports hall to roll out the 30-meter grid and photograph it. He is also on a quest to photograph all Japanese number plates whose four digits are lines in the times tables. 'I came out of a restaurant in Ginza [Tokyo's upmarket entertainment district] a couple of weeks ago and I saw two cars parked next to each other. The plates were 84 32 and 83 24!' he says (Just in case you missed it: 8 x 4 = 32, and 8 x 3 = 24). 'I was crying out of joy.'

In 1983 Kaji's magazine – full name *Puzzle Communication Nikoli* – published its first grid logic puzzle, Cross Sums, an arithmetical brainteaser that originated in the US in the fifties. He called it Kasan Kurosu – from the Japanese for 'addition' and the Japanese pronunciation of the English word 'cross' – which he later abbreviated to Kakuro. In 1984 he introduced Number Place, which had first appeared in the magazine *Dell Pencil Puzzles and Word Games* in the late seventies. He called this one Sudoku, which means 'the number appears only once'.

Kaji admired US puzzle magazines, and was trying to emulate their style. He judged his readers' tastes perfectly. Not only did they enjoy solving these number-based puzzles, but it also turned out that they were eager to create their own. When *Nikoli* introduced a section for readers' puzzles, it became the most popular part of the magazine. The first ideas for new puzzles that came in needed tweaking, but soon there was barely any need for staff involvement, since readers were themselves suggesting improvements and providing pages and pages of examples. *Nikoli* became a magazine almost entirely written by its readers, who were not only inventing new types of puzzle, but also supplying many examples of each type of puzzle for publication. So far, the magazine has introduced about 300 new puzzle types.

In most *Nikoli* puzzles, the solver is required to fill in a grid, typically by shading in cells, drawing a path or dividing the grid into regions. The rules are simple and intuitive, obeying certain conventions. For example, cells are only considered adjacent when they are horizontal and vertical neighbors, and loops never branch or intersect. Each step can be deduced logically from the ones before, and there is a unique solution. Reader feedback has provided a rigorous stress-test for honing the ideas. A puzzle has to make regular appearances in the 'new puzzles' section for a couple of years before it has the chance to ascend to *Nikoli*'s main pages. The puzzles I've selected for this book are polished gems, crowd-pleasers, accessible to everyone. The point of a good puzzle, says Kaji, is not education but entertainment. They must have a sense of humor and an element of surprise.

Kaji thinks *Nikoli*'s puzzles tap into national characteristics. 'The Japanese like logical thinking,' he says. 'We have a discipline of "try, try, and try again". In Europe and the USA it is always "fun, fun, fun".' He adds that the puzzles present you with a very structured path from easy ones to medium ones, and from medium to hard. The Japanese are very comfortable with thinking about life as a progression up a hierarchy. Working your way through the puzzles is a perfect metaphor for the career of a Japanese salaryman starting at the bottom and rising to the top.

With us is Jimmy Goto, who is an old school friend of Kaji's and *Nikoli*'s executive financial officer. He mentions the tradition of *hakoniwa*, miniature landscape gardens in a small box that many Japanese have in their homes, arranged with tiny plants and stones, often decorated with toy-sized bridges, houses and people. 'The Japanese like to miniaturise,' he says. 'Puzzles in small grids have the same feeling as *hakoniwa*.'

Nikoli, now a quarterly, was always a niche magazine – its circulation is only about 15,000 – and it was startling for Kaji that in 2005 he suddenly found international fame as the 'godfather' of Sudoku. The craze was a bonanza for his company, which for a short while was able to sell its puzzles all over the world, before most outlets found cheaper ways of producing them by computer. Kaji says he is glad he only achieved financial success when he was in his fifties, since if he had been younger he would probably have blown the lot on girls, booze and gambling. (Sudoku is still hugely popular in Japan, selling roughly 3 million books and magazines there each year. Ironically, most of these publications call the puzzle Number Place, because Kaji trademarked the name 'Sudoku' in Japan, and *Nikoli* now only represents a small share of the market.)

Every month *Nikoli* still receives about 4,500 puzzles – all submitted by post – from a core community of about 500 puzzle masters. The postbag contains about 50 ideas for new puzzles, a few of which will make the 'new puzzles' section. The rest are examples of the magazine's classic puzzles, which the creators make by writing out a final grid, then removing elements until they are left with a desirable starting position. They are all solved by staff members – a computer also checks that the solutions are unique – and the best ones chosen for publication.

Every puzzle in the magazine is always credited to its author, usually under his or her pen name, a tradition that *Nikoli* has encouraged (as has long been the custom for crosswords). Readers learn to recognize the different styles of the most frequent creators, who are the anonymous stars of the scene. Even though *Nikoli* relies on its creators, however, it knows very little about them – only their names, addresses and ages. Jimmy Goto says they are 80 per cent men, come from all over the country, and cover all ages from schoolchildren to seniors. The only opportunity *Nikoli* staff get to meet them is at the party the magazine hosts for them in Tokyo every year. The highlight of the evening is the *Nikoli* derby, a party game invented by a reader two decades ago. Each person writes their name, and a number of their own choosing, on a piece of paper. The aim is to choose the lowest number that no one else has also chosen. *Nikoli* staff gather the pieces of paper and place them one by one on a board. In the style of a horse-racing commentator, a narrator shouts out the numbers that appear, keeping the audience informed on the number currently in the winning position – that is, the lowest number that has appeared on only one piece of paper – until the number on the very last piece of paper reveals who is the winner.

The amount of reader participation means that *Nikoli* has a huge library of examples, at every level of difficulty. Staff grade the puzzles using symbols: smile (easy), frown (medium), cry (hard) and scream (very hard). Each puzzle has two standard sizes, usually a 10 x 10 grid and a 17 x 17 grid. To appreciate a puzzle you need several examples, which is why *Nikoli* always publishes its puzzles in groups of at least six, beginning with an 'easy' on a small grid – a shallow pool for dipping your toes in the water. In the following pages I have included 10 examples of each puzzle, always starting with two smiles.

Let's get to it!

Slitherlink スリザーリンク

LENIN, YUKI TODOROKI, *NIKOLI*, 1989

The challenge: Create a single loop by connecting horizontally and vertically adjacent dots with lines.

The rules: The loop must be unbroken, never cross itself, and have no branches. A number in a cell indicates the number of line segments that surround that cell. Empty cells may be surrounded by any number of lines.

How to solve it:

A. The starting grid.

B. In this chapter I'm going to use the word **freebie** for an opening move that requires almost no thinking. Freebies are treats placed by the creator to get you started. The freebies in this puzzle are the cells with a 0. By definition these cells have no line segments surrounding them, so we put little crosses in the spaces where we know there are no lines. One of the 0s has a 3 to its left and a 3 below it, leaving only three possible spaces around each of those 3s, so we can instantly draw in those lines, creating the first fragment of the loop.

C. At either end of the first fragment we can continue the loop only in one direction. The loop cannot branch or break, which means that if a dot is on the loop it has exactly two lines emerging from it. Consider the dot at the bottom left of the 3 in the second column. We know it is on the loop, since it has two lines coming from it, which means we can put little crosses to the left and below it where we know there can be no lines. By eliminating these lines, we can deduce that the 2-cell there must have its two lines on its left and bottom sides. Now look at the cells with a 2 on the top row and the rightmost

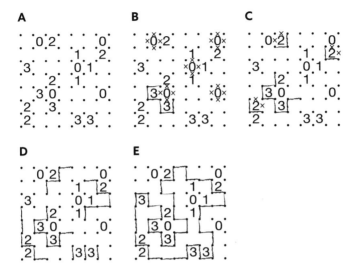

column that are adjacent to the 0-cells. We've already ruled out one line surrounding each 2. We can also rule out each line along the edge of the grid: in each case, if this line was filled in, it would be a branch off the loop, which is forbidden. (I've marked these no-go areas with a cross.) Only two possible lines remain for these 2-cells, so the ones I've marked must be the correct ones.

D. We can extend the new fragments a little, by drawing lines in the only places the ends can go before they reach a point where there's more than one possible route. But we can also make a helpful deduction about the two 3s on the bottom row. If the line between the two cells was left empty, that would determine the three sides of each 3-cell that require a line. But this would create a small, separate loop around both 3s, which is forbidden (the puzzle's solution must be a single loop). So the line between the 3s must be filled in. And if the line passes down the middle of two 3-cells, it must also pass through the two sides of the 3-cells that are parallel to that middle line, because if it didn't you would get branching from the loop.

E. Carry on extending the fragments wherever you can until the loop is complete. For example, the loop must carry on up the left side of the grid past the 3 in the first column, since if it took a right turn below the 3 it would end up (after three line segments) back on the left side of the grid with no way to join up with another fragment of the loop. And the line on the bottom edge of the grid must extend to the corner of the 3-cell on the bottom row, which means the loop must go over that 3-cell and under the one to its right, before rising and passing one cell left of the 0 on the rightmost column.

➡ When *Nikoli* launched its section for readers to submit their own puzzles, a teenage student using the pen name Lenin sent in one of the first ideas: a suggestion in which dots were placed around numbers in a grid. One of *Nikoli*'s staff members combined this idea with a suggestion from another reader, Yuki Todoroki, to create Slitherlink. Originally every cell had a number in it, until the compilers realized that you could leave some squares blank and still get a unique solution. Slitherlink was the earliest original Nikoli puzzle to become one of the flagships of the magazine.

What I love about Slitherlink is not only its elegance but also the way it is a literal interpretation of the idea that in life we are always looking for the path to the solution of any problem. Here the path is the solution! When I'm solving a Slitherlink, I feel like an adventurer journeying through a hidden world. The puzzle throws up many interesting patterns for how the loop must pass through different combinations of numbers.

As we're at the beginning of the book, here are a few tips: **A** shows that if a 1-cell is diagonally adjacent to a 0-cell, the loop cannot pass through their common corner. Tips **B** and **C** are a result of the fact that if a line goes to the corner of a 0-cell, then there must be a second line out of the corner cell, otherwise the line will end in a spike. Tip **D** arises because the dot common to two diagonally adjacent 3-cells must only connect a single line from each cell, to avoid branching.

A

B

C

D

ASUKORU

```
2 3      1    2 0
  0 2 1  3      2
        3 2  1
1   2  1      3 2
0 3      0 3
      2 3      3 3
3 0      1  3   2
    1  3 3
0      0  1 0 1
1 3    3      3 3
```

2 / CHIMIKANA

```
   0           3
3    3 1 3 3     3
    2        3
  2  3  3    2
  2        3  1
  0  1       2
  3    0  2  1
    2        2
3    0 3 1 3     3
  2           0
```

3 / 🥷🥷 MR. SCIENCE

```
2     0 1   0 2 3
  3 2     2
  1 3       1     2
3                 0
      2 0   2 3 2
1 2 2 2 1
3                 2
3     1       2 3
        3     0 3
3 3 2 3 1       2
```

4 / 🥷🥷 ROUTE TAKANA

```
        2 0 2   2
  3   2       3
  3     3   3 1   3
2             1   1
  1   3   1     2
  1       1   3   1
1   2             3
3   1 3   3     0
    0         3   3
  1   2 3 2
```

```
   3   1 2   2       3
2         3     3
   1   3 0         3
3           2 2   3
   3   1 2           0
1           1 2   3
   1   1 2           3
1           0 3   3
   3   1               3
3       3   3 2   3
```

```
2 2 2     3 3       1
   3       2       1 3
      1         3   3
3       3 1
2     3       3   3
   3   3       3       0
          1 3       1
2   3           2
3 3       1       3
2     1 2     3 2 3
```

7/ 🥷🥷 MASAKO KATSURAGAWA

```
  2 0 2    1 1         0        3 3    3 1 3
1      2      1 3   2   0 3      2         0
1      1    3 2           2 1    2       1
1      3    3      3 1 2      2      3       0
  2 1 1    3    1 2      2 0    2    3 1 2
          1    0 3      2 2    2
  1 2 0      2         0        2 2 3
  2   3  3 3   2     0      2   2 0   2   0
  2 0 1      1      0        2 3 2
          1    2 2      3 3    2
  3 3 1    3    2 1    2 0    3    1 3 3
2      3    1    3 0 1      1    1      1
3      1    2 2           2 2    1      2
3      3      3 0   3   0 3      2      1
  3 2 3    0 2      3        3 1    3 3 1
```

8/ 🥷🥷🥷 MYUNA

```
  2   3    1 3 3 2        3 2 3 2    2   1
2      3   3      2   2 3 0   2      0   3      3
0      2   1      1         2      3   0      3
  3   3    1 0 2 1   2 2 3   1 1 2 1    3   0

2 2   0 3 2 1 2    1 1 1 3 3    2 3 3 3 2   3 3
  3   2      2   1         0   1      1   2
  0   1      0   1         2   1      3   1
  1   3      3   3         1   2      3   2
1 1    1 2 3 1 1    2 1 3 1 0    2 3 1 2 2   2 0

  2   3    1 0 1 0   1 1 1   2 2 3 2    3   3
3      2   1      1         0   1   0      0
3      2   3      1   1 1 1   1      3   2      1
  3   1    3 1 1 3         2 2 1 3    0   3
```

```
1 2 0     3     3   3 3 3           3 3 3
      3       0     3         2 0 3
3   1   2     3     3                 2   2   3
1                       3 3 3         1   1   3
  3 3   3     3     2           3 3 3
            1       3                   2 0 2
            2       3       3 1 2
2 3 3   3 0 3                       3 2 3   3 3 3
          1 0 1           2     3
  2 0 3                   3     2
          0 3 1           3     0     3   3 3
0   3   1         1 3 3   3     3   0   2   3
1   2   0                 3     3               2
      3 3 3               0     3   3       0 2 3
  3 3 2             1 0 2   2     3       2 1   3
```

Hashiwokakero 橋をかけろ

LENIN, 1990

The challenge: Link islands (circles) with bridges (straight lines), so that the number on each island describes the number of bridges coming from that island.

The rules: A maximum of two bridges can join any two islands. Bridges must be either horizontal or vertical, and cannot cross other islands or bridges. The bridges must form a continuous link between all islands.

How to solve it:

A. The starting grid.

B. **Freebies:** The 4-island at the top left must have four bridges. It's in a corner, so there are only two possible islands it can join. Since it cannot join to either with more than two bridges, it must join to both with two. The 3-island in the top right must have three bridges. The options are two horizontal bridges and one vertical, or one horizontal bridge and two vertical. Either way, it must have *at least one* horizontal and *at least one* vertical. Every 8-island is a gift. The maximum number of bridges for any island is 8, so when we see an 8-island we can connect it with two bridges in each of the four directions.

C. The 4-island nestling near the top-right corner also has its bridges determined: two horizontal and two vertical. The 4-island on the bottom must link with a single bridge to each 1-island: if it linked with more than one bridge to a 1-island, then that 1-island would have multiple bridges, which is forbidden. The bridges that have now been marked restrict the positions of the remaining bridges, making up the final grid.

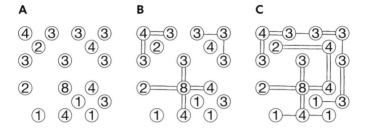

➤ *Nikoli's* reader's corner was a huge success and its early hits were due in large part to the puzzlist Lenin. He came up with the idea for Hashiwokakero, which means 'Let's cross the bridge'. You don't even need to know about graph theory to enjoy these puzzles. (Graph theory is the study of objects and how they link together; among other things it is used in studying the maths of social networks. A graph theorist would describe a completed Hashiwokakero puzzle as a connected graph in which each node has at most two edges.)

The key thought process in solving these puzzles is to realize that bridges always connect two islands – in other words, when you introduce a new bridge from one island you are not only increasing that island's bridges by one but also those of the island you are connecting to. The rule that the islands must all be joined together in a continuous link – which means that you could walk from any island to any other across bridges – is crucial to solving the more complicated grids.

① ① ② ③ ④
① ② ③ ③

② ③ ② ③
② ①
① ④ ⑦ ④

③ ④ ⑥ ②
② ③ ③ ③ ③

4 / YURI HASEGAWA

5 / YURI HASEGAWA

6 / METASEQUOIA

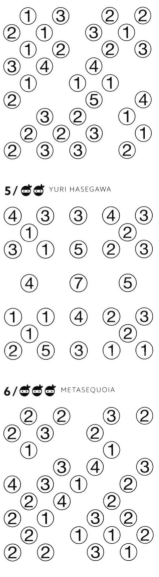

7/ METASEQUOIA

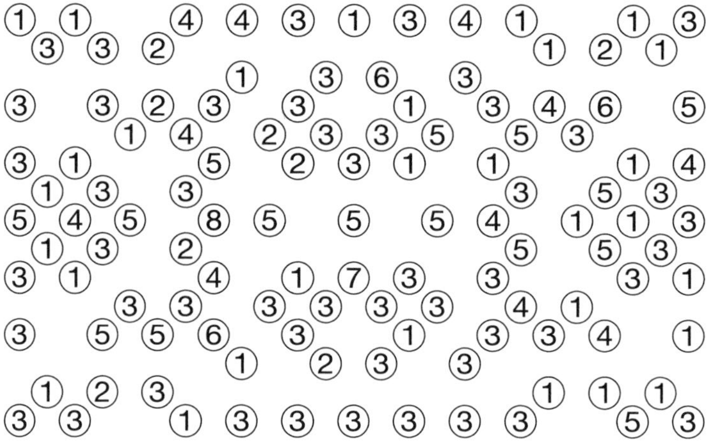

8/ TOSHIO KARINO

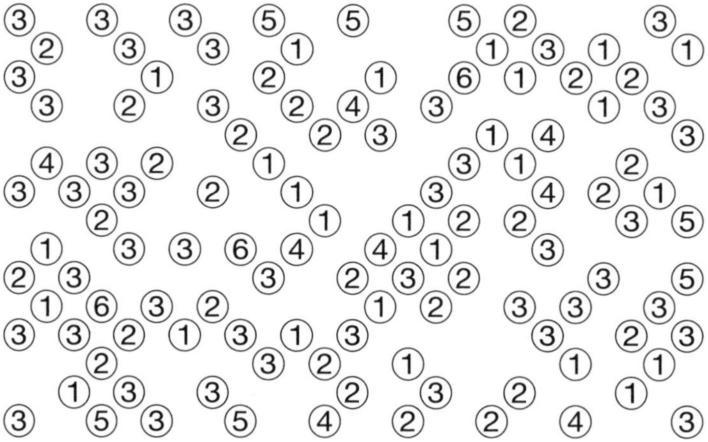

9 / METASEQUOIA

10 / TOSHIO KARINO

Nurikabe ぬりかべ

LENIN, 1991

The challenge: Shade in certain cells to create 'islands' of white/ empty cells. The numbers denote the white cells necessary to make up each 'island'.

The rules: White cells in an 'island' are connected horizontally or vertically. You cannot shade in a cell containing a number, and each 'island' has only one number. The 'river' of shaded-in cells between the 'islands' must form a single contiguous region in which its cells are connected either horizontally or vertically. No 2 x 2 square of four cells may be entirely shaded in.

How to solve it:

A. The starting grid.

B. **Freebies:** We can isolate the single-cell islands, which are those cells containing a 1, by shading in the four cells horizontally and vertically adjacent to them. No island ever has two numbers in it, so if a single cell separates two numbers we can shade that one in, as I have done in the top row between the 2 and the 3 and in the sixth row between the 2 and the 2. If two numbered cells share a common corner, such as the 5 in the bottom row and the 2 above it to the right, we can shade in the other two squares that share that common corner, since otherwise these two numbers would be in the same island, which is forbidden.

C. Think white! We can complete the 2-island in the top-left corner, because the only cell connected horizontally or vertically to the 2-cell is the one below it, marked with a dot. Once we have completed an island we can then isolate it by shading in the cells horizontally and vertically adjacent to it. Likewise, the cell marked with a dot above the 2 in the bottom

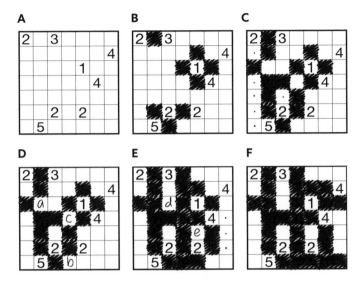

A   B   C

D   E   F

left must be white, completing that island, which we isolate with shaded cells. Once we have completed these two islands, we can deduce that the 5-island must run up the left side of the grid, again marked with dots, and we shade a final cell in the second column, fourth row to enclose it.

D. Think shade! Look at the cells marked **a** and **b**. These cells must both be shaded, otherwise they would each leave a single shaded cell disconnected from the other shaded cells, contradicting the rule that the river of shaded cells is a single contiguous region. The cell **c** must also be shaded, since it is isolated from all other white cells, but it doesn't contain a number, so it can't be an island.

E. Here we use the final rule. The cells marked **d** and **e** cannot be shaded, as this would contravene the rule banning 2 x 2 blocks of shaded cells. And if **d** is white, then the 3-island must be those three vertically connected cells; if **e** is white, the 2-island is also completed. We can now shade in around the new islands to isolate them. I have also marked with dots the only possible position of the lower 4-island.

F. The completed grid. Note that the top 4-island must contain the top-right cell, since if it didn't the shaded cell in that position would be disconnected from the other shaded cells, which is forbidden.

➡ The name of this puzzle comes from the *nurikabe*, a Japanese folk spirit that manifests itself as an invisible wall. What I find so alluring is that it feels like two puzzles in one. When solving a Nurikabe, you must flip back and forth from seeing it as a puzzle about a river to a puzzle about islands. At any point you inevitably have one of two perspectives: are you following where the river will flow, or are you thinking about where the dry land must be? Both mindsets are different, and it is easy to get too focused on one, forgetting that you will only make progress if you switch to the other. The tension between these two perspectives is thrilling.

Nurikabe, which first appeared in the magazine in 1991, was also the third and final classic *Nikoli* puzzle thought up by Lenin. After a burst of activity as a puzzle inventor and creator, however, Lenin later drifted away from the magazine. 'Lenin is one of the most mysterious creators,' says Jimmy Goto. 'Twenty years ago, we had contact with him every day. No one has had contact with him now for five or six years.'

7			9					
	4						4	
								6
6								
	3					2		
				3			2	

2/ KNY

7		3				2		
							3	
			4					
4			1					
				3				1
				5				
	3							
		4				1		3

3/ OGAWA-MINORI

				2					
	1				2		2		4
		3							
3		4				3			
5								3	
							4		
5								4	

4/ E-ZAWAZAWA

							2		4
				2					
							1		4
7		3							
					3				
14		8							

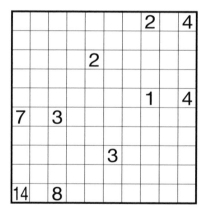

4			2			3	
3			4			2	
			4			3	
	2			4			
	1			2			2
	4			3			3

6 / SHINMAKE

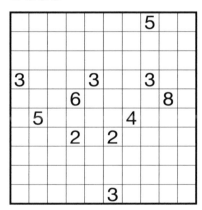

						5		
3			3			3		
		6					8	
	5				4			
		2		2				
			3					

		7								5		
3			4				3				5	
									7			
3												7
								3				
	2											
4												
												3
			6		3					4		
	2			4			9		4			
4												4
	4			2			1			3		
	6									3	1	
	3						4		6			

8 / 🥷🥷🥷 KABASHISAMA

				5					4			3				
			2							3					5	
3				5												6
	5															
							4									
						3										
													5			
					5		3			6						
						4					3					2
									2							
4																
	4															
								4								
													4			
6												3			5	
	4												5			3
						3		3								

31

9/ GUTEN

1	2	3	4	5	6	7	8	9	10	11	12	13	14	15	16
				3							2				
	4				3							2			3
4														4	
					3				4						
			4			4									
												5			
															2
				5				4							
							6					4			
2				4	4					3				3	
	2												2		
					4										
			4				3				4			2	
4								3							2
												3			
		1		3	4						2				

10/ 😈😈😈😈 KS

			5				3			4		5	
	3					2							
2													
											3		2
						4						4	
							4						
										2			
	7		6		7								
1													4
								5			6	2	
			7										
							3						
	2							4					
1		4											
													2
								3				7	
	1		2				7			2			

Heyawake へやわけ

HIROYUKI FUKUSHIMA, 1992

The challenge: The grid is divided into 'rooms', some of which contain a number. Shade cells so that the number in each room describes the number of cells in that room that are shaded.

The rules: No two shaded cells can be horizontally or vertically adjacent. A horizontal or vertical line of white cells cannot pass through more than two rooms. All white cells must be linked together to form a single region that is connected horizontally or vertically. Rooms with no numbers in them may or may not contain shaded cells.

How to solve it:
A. The starting grid.
B. **Freebies:** A one-cell room containing a 1 can be shaded in straight away. A three-cell room with a 2 in it can only be shaded one way, since shaded cells cannot be horizontally or vertically adjacent to one another. Less obviously, a four-cell room in a corner with a 2 in it can also only be shaded one way. Look at the room in the top-right corner. We know that the two shaded cells cannot be horizontally or vertically adjacent, so they must be diagonally adjacent, either stacked in the \ direction or in the / direction. We can rule out the former because this would trap a white cell in the top-right corner of the grid, which contradicts the rule that all white cells must be connected to one another.
C. The trickiest rule to get the hang of is the one that says that a line of white cells cannot pass through more than two rooms. We can use that rule for the cell marked **a**. We know there can't be shaded cells in the column beneath **a** because both the rooms it passes through have a 0. But if **a** is unshaded then

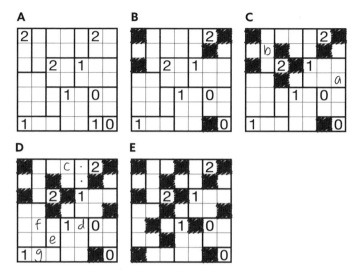

there is a vertical line of cells, the bottom four cells of the right column, that passes through more than two rooms. From the bottom, the line passes up through the two rooms with a 0 and into a third room, the one **a** is in. So **a** must be shaded in.

Now look at **b**. It cannot be shaded in, since this would block off a white cell, which is forbidden, since all white cells must be connected. Using the rule that you cannot have a line of white cells passing through more than two rooms, we can deduce that the cell to the right of **b** must be shaded in, which in turn means that the cell below this shaded cell (with the 2 in it) must be empty. This then forces the positions of the two shaded cells in that 2-room.

D. Neither of the cells in the room marked with two dots can be shaded in, because either the white cell with the 2 will be isolated, or because the cell is adjacent to one already shaded in. The only permissible shading position remaining on the top row that avoids a white line passing through more than two rooms is **c**. Likewise, we must shade in **d** to stop a vertical white line passing through more than two rooms (because we know the cells above it passing two rooms are empty). With **d** shaded in we can shade in **e** to stop a horizontal white line passing through more than two rooms (because we know the cells to the right of it passing through two rooms are empty). Which means we can shade in **f** too, since the two cells to its right cannot now be shaded and they pass through two rooms. The single shaded cell in the room on the bottom row that contains a 1 cannot be **g**, since that would split the white area into two. So it must be the bottom-left corner cell.

E.   The completed grid.

➥ Heyawake comes from the words *heya*, room, and *wake*, divide. Although I sometimes read it as 'Hey! AWAKE!', because it is one of the more challenging *Nikoli* puzzles, and it has kept me awake at night. Even though the rules are a little bit more complicated than some of the other puzzles, I like the emptiness of the grid, the way you often feel that there is not enough information to make the next move, and the pleasingly minimalist 2-tone solutions, which a ska singer might choose for their bathroom tiles.

One useful strategy is to start at the edges. You can rule out shading cells that hem in a white cell on an edge, since any white cell on an edge must be connected to the other white cells. Big numbers are also sometimes helpful, since there are only certain ways to fill certain rooms – for example, there is only one way to shade five cells in a 3 x 3 room, as illustrated here.

1/ AWAYUKI MIZORE

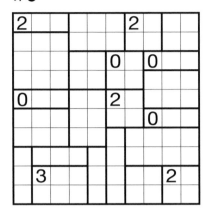

2/ MASAKO KATSURAGAWA

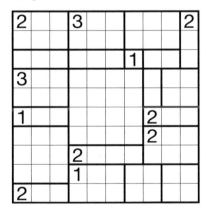

3 / 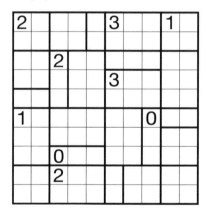 3-JI KANSU

					2		
2							
			2				
		2			**2**		
			2			**2**	
2							
			2				
2							

4 / HAKUGIN-NO-OOKAMI

2				**3**		**1**	
	2						
			3				
1					**0**		
	0						
2							

38

5 / YUMA MIYAIJ

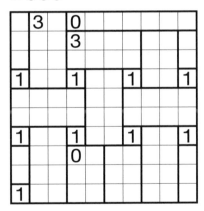

6 / WARE-HITO-NI-ARAZU

7/ HIROO KAWADU

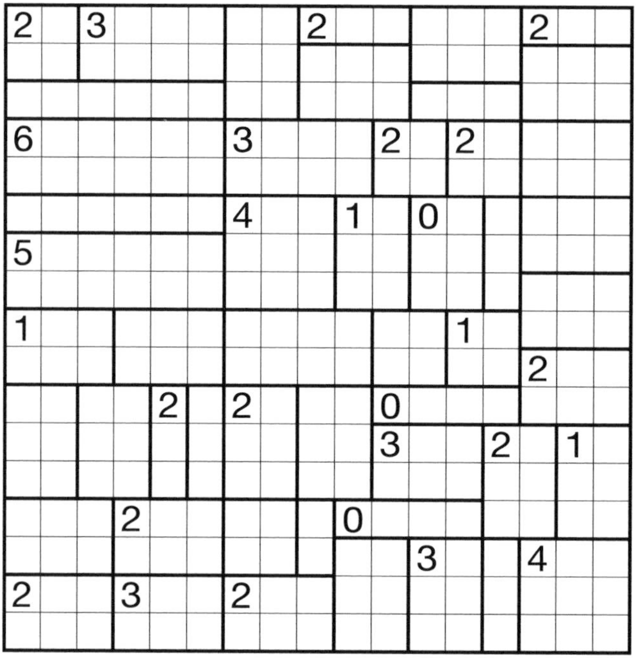

9/ CHIMIKANA

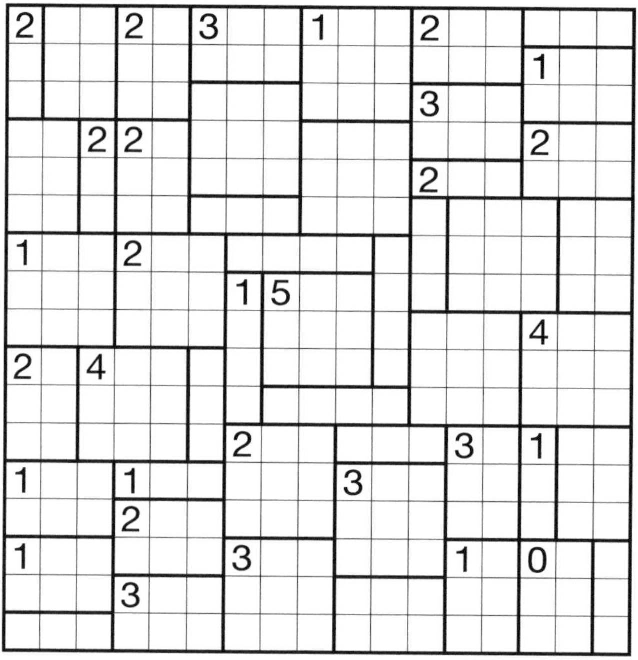

Fillomino フィルオミノ

SURANTA, 1994

The challenge: Divide the grid into blocks that have the same number in every cell, so that the number is also the number of cells in the block.

The rules: A block with a 1 will have a single cell. A block made up of 2s will have two cells; a block made from 3s will have three cells; and so on. Blocks are made up of cells that are adjacent horizontally and/or vertically. Two blocks containing the same number cannot touch horizontally or vertically, but they can touch diagonally. Some blocks may have no given numbers in the opening grid.

How to solve it:

A. The starting grid.

B. **Freebies:** Each cell with a 1 is its own block, so draw in its boundary. Now look at the 7 in the top-left corner. It must be part of a block with seven cells. There is only one way for the block to fill out, since two of its sides are restricted by 5s. We can add a new 7 to the left of the given 7, and draw two more 7s below it. We'll come back to the 7s later, but meanwhile we have a similar situation with the 4 in the bottom right. There is only one way for that block to fill out, climbing up the side column. Once we have added three 4s to the given 4, the block is complete. Likewise, we can add a 5 next to the 5 in the top row, and a 7 next to the 7 in the bottom row. In the bottom left, a 2 cannot go in position **a** since this would create a block of three 2s, which is forbidden. So there is only one place for the second 2, which completes the block containing the bottom-left cell.

A

```
7 5 . . . 2
5 1 . . . .
. . . 5 . 4
2 . 3 . . .
. . . 1 7 .
2 . . . 7 4
```

B

```
7 7 5 5 . 2
7 5 1 . . .
7 . . . 5 . 4
2 . 3 . . 4
a . . . 1 7 4
2 2 . 7 7 4 4
```

C

```
7 7 5 5 . 2
7 5 1 . . .
7 5 . . 5 . 4
7 7
2 2 3 . . 7 4
. . . . 1 7 4
2 2 . 7 7 4 4
```

D

```
7 7 5 5 5 5 2
7 5 1 · · 5
7 5 5 5 5 . 4
7 7 7 . . . b
2 2 3 . . 7 4
. . . 1 7 4
2 2 . 7 7 4 4
```

E

```
7 7 5 5 5 5 2
7 5 1 2 2 5 2
7 5 5 5 5 4 4
7 7 7 d 4 4 1
2 2 3 7 7 7 4
9 e . c 1 7 4
2 2 f 7 7 4 4
```

F

```
7 7 5 5 5 5 2
7 5 1 2 2 5 2
7 5 5 5 5 4 4
7 7 7 1 4 4 1
2 2 3 7 7 7 4
1 3 3 7 1 7 4
2 2 1 7 7 4 4
```

C. When one block starts to fill up, it often forces the position of another block. The 7s in the top left force the 5 in the second row to 'grow' downwards, which itself forces the position of two more 7s, which means we can complete the 2-block on the fifth row. And the 4s in the bottom right force the 7 in the second-bottom row to 'grow' upwards.

D. We complete the top-left 7-block, forcing an extra two 5s in the third row, which join the given 5 to complete that block. The 5-block in the top row must continue along the top row and avoid the cells with a dot, since no two blocks with the same number can be horizontally or vertically adjacent. The two dots must be a block of 2s. Now you get to enjoy the sense of the grid practically filling itself in. There is only one way to complete the 2-block in the top right. The cell **b** cannot be a 4, otherwise two 4-blocks would touch, so the uncompleted 4-block must zig-zag around that cell, which must be a 1.

E. The 7-block must include cell **c**, since there is no other way to complete the block, confirming **d** as a 1-block. The given 3 is in a block that either extends to **e** or **f**. If it extends to **f**, we are left with only **e** and **g**. This pair cannot be in a 2-block, since this would put them adjacent to not one but two other 2-blocks. Nor can they be two 1-blocks, since this would put two 1-blocks next to one another, which is forbidden. So the 3-block must extend to **e**, and **g** and **f** are 1s.

F. The completed grid.

➥ Fillomino is the only major *Nikoli* puzzle apart from Sudoku and Kakuro that requires the solver to write numbers in a grid. In Sudoku, however, the numbers are just symbols – meaning they have no value as numbers: you could use any nine shapes. What I enjoy about Fillomino is that the numerical value is important, and I find the self-reference – the way that each number correctly describes the size of its block – very satisfying. The name Fillomino unfortunately has nothing to do with the Philippines or fillies. It comes from the mathematical language used to describe blocks of identical squares joined horizontally or vertically. Dominoes are made from two connected squares, triominoes from three, tetrominoes from four, and so on, with polyominoes the general term. The aim of Fillomino is to **fill** the grid with poly**omino**es. These puzzles can get quite tricky, and to find the next move you often need to go away for a while and come back with fresh eyes.

8		1				1		
2				1		2	6	5
	4	2	1				7	
					2			1
	3			4			1	4
2	2				1		4	
1			3					
		3			1	6	2	
	2	2	1		3			3
		8				6		5

5	6			6	6			7
5				6	1			2
5	5			6		1		
5	3		6					
					6		7	1
	3		2				7	5
4			6	5				1
4			4	5			5	5

3 / 🥷🥷 KUDAGITSUNE

1		4		4				3
2		2		2				4
3		3		4				1
6		6		2				5
	4		1			5		
		4			5		3	
4		6		6				3
4		4		5				1
4		3		3				3
6		6		6				2

4 / 🥷🥷 COFFEE BEANS

4			4	2	5	3			5
	2		1			3		5	
		3	3			1	3		
3	2	5					1	6	2
5									2
5									6
5	4	4					6	2	4
	2	1				4	4		
	3		2			1		4	
2			4	4	3	5			5

5 / 🐱🐱 NAOKI MIYAJI

4	4							
3	3		4	4				
2	4		3	2			2	4
			4	4			4	3
							1	3
3	4							
1	2		2	4				
4	3		3	2			2	3
			4	3			3	3
							4	4

6 / 🐱🐱🐱 OTOBOKE MOGURA

5						4	
4	4	2	1		4	3	
5						4	
1		5	5	6	6		6
6		6	3	6	1		1
2						1	
6	1	4	1		4	6	
4						4	

```
      3 7 4           4 7 1
      4   2           7   2
      3   7           2   1
3 4 4         7 3 1 4 2         2 6 3
5                 7                   4
7 5 7         2 7 2 4 7         5 2 1
      1   7           4   2
      2   7           7   3
      5 2 3           2 7 4
      3   3           3   3
      1   6           3   3
7 6 6         3 3 7 2 7         2 4 1
3                 3                   7
2 5 6         6 2 5 2 7         1 5 3
      5   4           5   2
      4   2           1   5
      5 4 3           2 7 3
```

5			1	2	3	4	1	2	3	4	5				6
	3		4								3		2		
		4				1					3				
	3		3		3		4			1		3			
7			5		2			3		3				3	
6				4				3					3		
5			5		7			4		3			4		
4			4			6		6			4		6		
3		3				5				6		4			
4			4			5		2		3		6			
5			5		2			5		3		6			
6				5				4				4			
7			2		6			5		4		6			
	2		4			1		4			3		3		
		5					4				1				
	2		6							4		4			
6			3	3	2	4	2	3	5	4	3				3

		3					7	7	7					4	
4	2	4			2	2				2	2		5	3	4
							7	7	7						
	1	2	5		2	2				2	2	5	2	3	
	2		2				7	7	7			7		1	
	5	2	5		2	2				2	2	4	7	3	
							7	7	7						
3	5	5			2	2				2	2		3	4	1
4		4					7	7	7				5		4
5	2	5			2	2				2	2		7	2	1
							7	7	7						
	5	6	4		2	2				2	2	7	3	5	
	3		3				7	7	7			3		2	
	2	4	2		2	2				2	2	5	3	4	
							7	7	7						
2	4	7			2	2				2	2		2	3	4
	2						7	7	7				6		

2	2	3	3	3	3	3	5	5	5
3	1	1	6	7	3 2 6	5 5			5
4	3	3	3						5
	1	1	1	3	8 2 3	5 5			
5	3	3	3						5
	5	1	6	3	1 8 1	5 5			
5									4
	5 6 5 6		3		1	3 5 8 7			
5									7
	1 3 1 3 1		5	4	1	1			
5					8	8	8		7
	1 3 1 3 1		5	1	1	1			
5					8	8	8		3
5	5 3 1 3 2	2	1	1	1				3
4	2 1	1	1	4	8	4 8			3

53

Yajilin ヤジリン

NEKOYAMA-TENPO, 1999

The challenge: Shade in some cells, and draw a single loop that passes through the grid. Every free cell must either be shaded or contain part of the loop.

The rules: If a cell contains a number and an arrow, then there must be exactly that number of shaded cells in the direction of the arrow before the edge of the grid. Shaded cells cannot be horizontally or vertically adjacent. The loop must be unbroken, never cross itself and have no branches. There may be shaded cells that don't have an arrow pointing to them. The cells containing numbers and arrows cannot be shaded, nor can the loop pass through them.

How to solve it:

A. The starting grid.

B. **Freebies:** Look at the 1-cell pointing up that is only a cell away from the edge. We can start by shading in the cell above it. Likewise, the 2-cell that is pointing horizontally three cells from the edge forces the positions of the shaded cells, since no two shaded cells can be horizontally adjacent. We can also start drawing the loop. The 0-cell reveals that the cell in the bottom-left corner cell is not shaded, so it must contain the loop, and there is only one way that the loop can go through it. When you start drawing the loop, draw a line in segments from the middle of a cell to the middle of an adjacent cell.

C. We can extend the loop from the bottom-left corner, being careful to extend it only to where we know it must go. The end in the left column must continue up that column, because if it turned horizontally, it would immediately block the other end on the bottom row. It rises up the left column by only

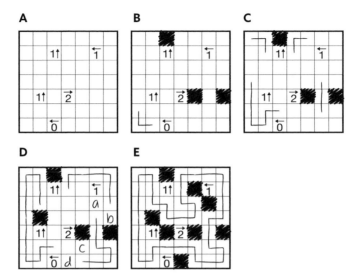

two cells, since at this stage we cannot deduce where it goes beyond that. We can draw other fragments of the loop too. The rules state that every cell is either shaded or contains part of the loop. So, since the third cell on the top row is shaded, the loop must pass through the second and the fourth cells, and there is only one way it can do this. Now look at the fifth row: the loop must pass through the empty cell between the two shaded ones.

D. By extending the loop into cells where we know it has to go (because there is nowhere else for it to continue), we reduce the options for shaded cells, such as the shaded cells in the second row and second column, which now have their positions determined. The loop must pass through **b**, since it cannot be shaded (as it is above a shaded cell), which links two fragments together. This means that **a** must be shaded, since there is no way for the loop to pass through that cell. The loop must pass through either **c** or **d**. But since **c** cannot be shaded in (because it is adjacent to a shaded cell), the loop must pass through **c**, and **d** must be shaded.

E. The finished grid.

➡ Yajilin, which means 'arrow-link', is perhaps the quintessential *Nikoli* puzzle, since it is a combination of two of the magazine's favored genres: shading-in puzzles and loop-drawing puzzles. It combines these genres while obeying the standard *Nikoli* rules that shaded-in squares cannot be horizontally or vertically adjacent, and there must be only one unbroken and unbranching loop. I find Yajilin particularly satisfying to complete because the grid starts off very empty, but by the end your pencil will have drawn something in every empty cell. If you start with the easy ones, gradually you learn the patterns of empty cells into which lines will fit, and the dead-ends where lines cannot go. In the larger grids, an arrow cell can point through another arrow cell. In all cases the number refers to the number of shaded cells before the edge of the grid.

1/🥷 SUBARU SAITO

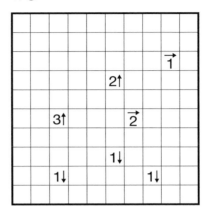

2/🥷 MASSU

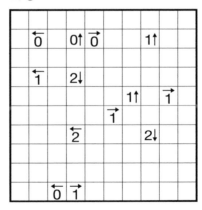

3 / 🥷🥷 IKOI-NO-MORI

	←0					1↑	
			1↑	→1			
			←2	2↓	1↑		
							0↓
			1↓				
	←1						
			0↓		←1		
					←1		

4 / 🥷🥷 AUXIN

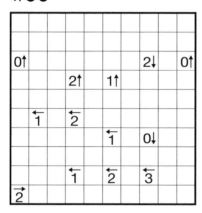

0↑					2↓	0↑	
		2↑	1↑				
	←1	←2					
			←1	0↓			
	←1	←2	←3				
→2							

5 / 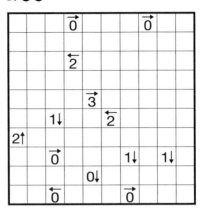 MR. SCIENCE

6 / KATSUKAZAN

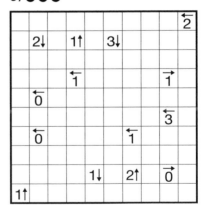

						1↑								
	←1								→3					
			2↑											
						→2								
			←3				1↓		→2			1↑		
					←1									
		2↑							←2					
1↑				←1					→3		→2			
						4↓								
		←2	1↓								2↓			
									0↓			1↓		
			←2											
										1↓				
		←2										→1		
			1↓							1↓				

8/ YASUDAKEI

	0↓	5↓	0↓	5↓	2↓	4↓	2↓								←2	
															←4	
												1↑			←2	
															←3	
			←2			2↑				3↑					←3	
		3↓											2↓		←3	
					2↓		←2								←2	
	→5										→3					
	→2				←2											
	→0								2↑							
	→4															
	→2			2↓									2↑			
	→3															
	→2								4↑	3↑	1↑	3↑	3↑	3↑	0↑	

9/ KUROTENTO

							1↑		→1							
						←2				→3						
								0↑								
						→2				→2						
								0↑								
		←0		3↑								0↑		2↑		
	←1				4↓						←3				1↑	
			←0										0↑			
	←0				3↓						←3				0↓	
		3↓		←2								1↓		1↓		
								→0								
						←2				→0						
								→3								
						←2				→0						
							→1		→0							

Masyu ましゅ

ACETONITRILE, RYUO YANO, 2000

The challenge: Draw a single loop that goes through every black circle and every white circle.

The rules: The loop must go **straight through every white circle**, and in at least one cell either just before or just after that white circle, the loop must turn 90 degrees. The loop must **turn 90 degrees at each black circle** and go straight through the cells either side of that black circle. The loop is a single loop: it must be unbroken, never cross itself, have no branches, nor pass through the same cell twice. The loop does not need to pass through all cells.

How to solve it:

A. The starting grid.

B. **Freebies:** The path of the loop can only go one way through single white circles on the edge, since it must go straight through them. So we can draw a line through those circles, making them look like London Underground symbols. (When drawing a line through two adjacent cells, always draw them between the centers of the cells.) There is also only one way to go through two adjacent white circles on the edge: straight through both of them. Since black circles must contain the corner of a 90-degree turn, there is only one way to go through a corner black circle.

C. Next, try to establish the path through the white circles. Where the path has arrived in a corner cell, there is only one way for it to proceed, so continue the path to the next cell. Remember, there is a helpful rule about white circles: in at least one of the cells before or after the loop passes through the circle it must turn 90 degrees. Look at the white circle in the leftmost

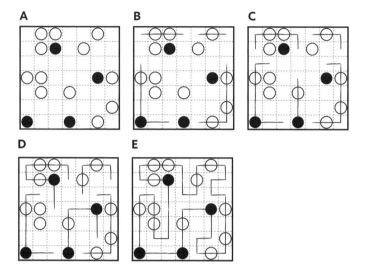

A **B** **C**

D **E**

column: the loop carries straight down below it. So, in the cell above that white circle, the loop must turn 90 degrees. Now look at the rightmost column, third cell down: the loop must turn 90 degrees here. We can also deduce that when a line passes through two adjacent circles, as it does in the top row, at either side of the circles there must be a 90-degree turn.

Now consider the black circle in the middle of the bottom row. The path of the loop through that circle can have only two options: either a 9 o'clock or a 3 o'clock position. We don't yet know which. Either way, though, the vertical line is common to both, so we can draw it in. It passes through the cell above the black circle, and reaches the white circle. This means we can continue it through the white circle, since lines go straight through white circles.

D. Now consider how the loop must pass through the black circle in the fourth row. The loop can't continue upwards from the black circle because that would create a T-junction in the cell immediately above it, which is forbidden since this effectively creates a branch. Neither can you continue the loop to the right of the black circle as it would intersect a fragment of the loop (creating two branches) and leave the grid. So the loop must head leftwards and downwards from the black circle. We can now deduce what happens at the black circle on the bottom row. If the loop heads rightwards, connecting with the loop through the white circle, then the fragment coming down from the black circle in the fourth row is prevented from rejoining the loop, which is not allowed. So the loop must go leftwards from the black circle on the bottom row. There is then only one way that all the remaining loose ends can join up to form a single loop.

E. The completed grid.

➡ Masyu's opening grid looks like the black-and-white counters on a Go board, although the similarity to the ancient Chinese board game is entirely coincidental. Originally the puzzle was called Pearl Necklace, and involved only white circles. The introduction of the black circles in 2000 made it more challenging and interesting, and it was renamed Black Pearls and White Pearls. But this was later changed when Maki Kaji misread the *kanji* character for pearl as 'masyu', which has no meaning. His colleagues found it hilarious that a man of his seniority was unable to read a character every primary school child knows.

One of the things I like about Masyu is its economy of form: it is one of the very few logic puzzles that has no numbers at all on the grid. I also like the look of the puzzle as you progress. The first lines originate from the black-and-white circles, which makes them feel like shoots sprouting from black-and-white seeds, the grid a petri dish. The unfinished grid looks spiky, poking you to finish the puzzle. Despite its simple rules, the puzzle is deceptively tricky. It is very easy to make a mistake, and to extend the line the wrong way. Be careful!

1/ MAKOTO TAKAHASHI

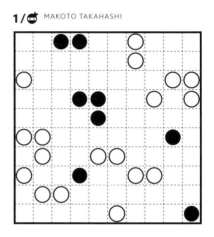

2/ NOBUHIRO TSUBOYA

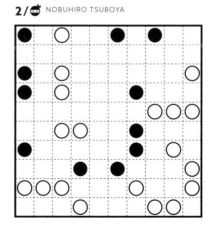

3 / 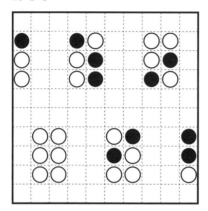 DENDEN-GUSA

4 / NISHIN

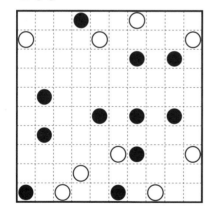

5 / 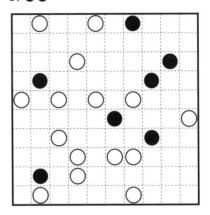 HERISHIKUTA

6 / 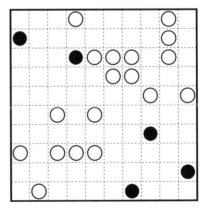 TATUYA FUJISAKI

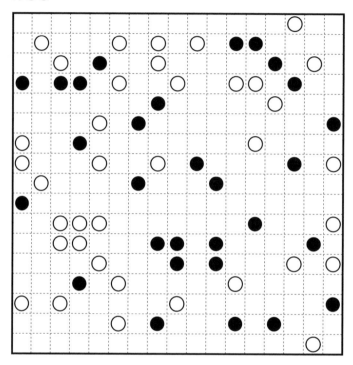

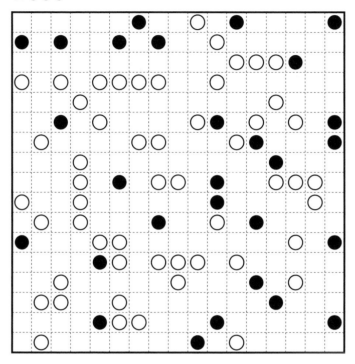

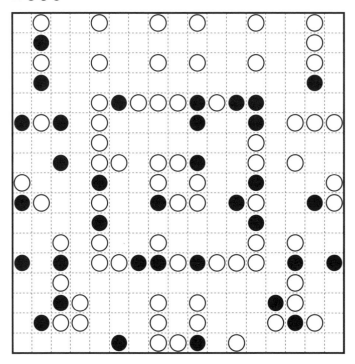

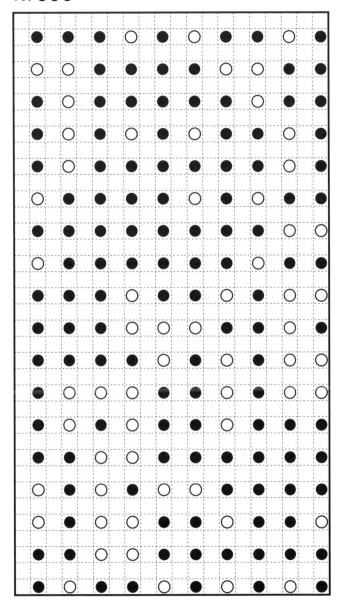

Tentai Show 天体ショー

GESAKU, 2001

The challenge: Divide the grid into regions. Each region must contain a single black or white dot. Each region must also be able to rotate 180 degrees around its dot and fit perfectly over its original position. (For example, when you rotate the letters I, H or X by 180 degrees around their central points, they will fit perfectly over their original positions, but the letters A, B and C will not.)

The rules: Create the regions by drawing solid lines over the dotted ones in the grid. Once you have divided the grid into regions, shade the regions that contain black dots to reveal a picture.

How to solve it:

A. The starting grid.

B. **Freebies:** Each region must contain its own dot. So if two adjacent cells contain a dot, the line between them must be a border line and can be marked.

C. Every region has two-fold rotational symmetry around its dot, meaning that if we were to rotate any region by half a revolution (or 180 degrees) about its dot, the region will fit perfectly over its original position. In other words, when we rotate a region 180 degrees, its top edge will become its bottom edge, and vice versa, and its left edge will become its right edge, and vice versa. Let's begin by rotating edges and seeing where they fall. Look at the cells with a dot that already have one of their sides marked. If the top side of a dot-cell is marked, we can mark the bottom side – and vice versa, since the top side will become the bottom side when rotated by 180 degrees. Likewise, if a left side is marked we can mark the right side, and vice versa.

D. The cell marked **a** must be in the region with the white dot to its

74

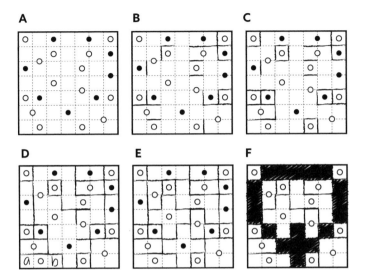

right, since there is no way for it to be in the orbit of any other dot except that white dot. By rotating the three marked sides of **a** by 180 degrees around the white dot, we can deduce that the cell marked **b** completes the region. Likewise, we can look at the sides of other partially completed regions and rotate them by 180 degrees. For example, look at the cell with the black dot five rows down and six cells along from the side of the grid. The left edge of this cell must also be on the (right) edge of the region that includes the white dot immediately to this cell's left. Rotate this edge by 180 degrees around the white dot, and mark where it lands. The way to make progress in this puzzle is to home in on the lines that you know must be on the edge of a region that contains a particular dot. These lines, however, are not always obvious. Remember that when you are building one edge of a region, you are automatically building the opposite edge too. As you complete each region, more clues emerge for those regions that contain the remaining dots.

E. The completed grid.

F. Shade in the regions containing black dots to reveal a picture.

➡ There is so much to love about this puzzle. First, its name is a bilingual triple pun. The Japanese word *ten-taisyo* means 'symmetry about a point', while the word *tentai* means 'heavenly body', such as a star. Tentai Show is thus an anglicized pronunciation of point symmetry with a double meaning of 'astronomical show' – which is brilliantly fitting since the dots in the grid really are like stars spinning in their orbits. Second, talking of stars, *viz* the Sun, the single-cell regions look pleasingly like the Japanese flag. Third, the puzzle feels especially dynamic, since in order to think in terms of rotational symmetry you are always spinning regions, like propellers, in your head. Finally, the puzzle is doubly satisfying to solve since you reveal a picture at the end, like completing a jigsaw. (In the image on the previous page, the picture is a necklace, or perhaps a flower. When the grids are larger the pictures are a lot more interesting, I promise!) Tentai Show combines logic with aesthetics, blurring the line between puzzles and art.

1 / SUNA-SAND & OXIO

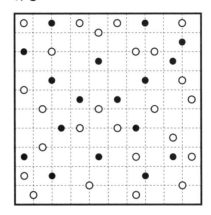

2 / YAKINCHU

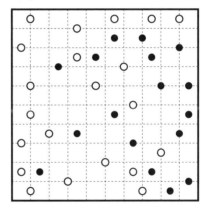

3 / MONCHY

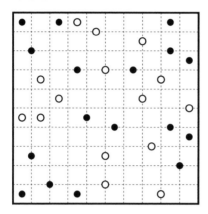

4 / COPEL-KUN

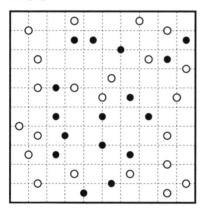

5 / KABASHISAMA

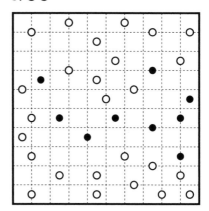

6 / KATORYU

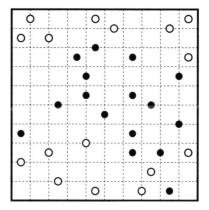

7/ 🐱🐱 NEKODUKI HINATA

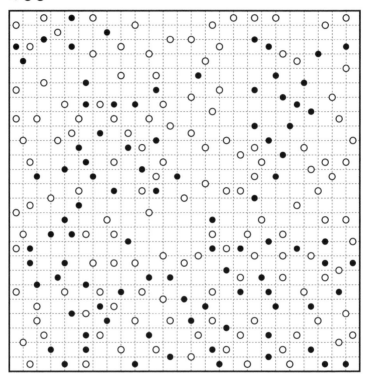

80

8 / 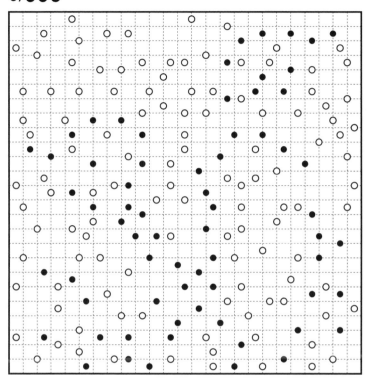 COMMON TIME

COMMON TIME

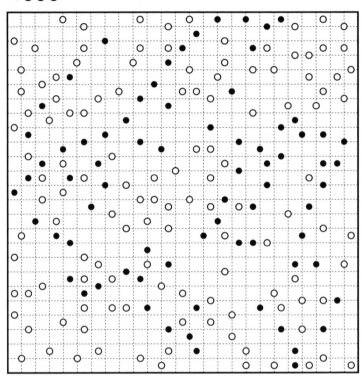

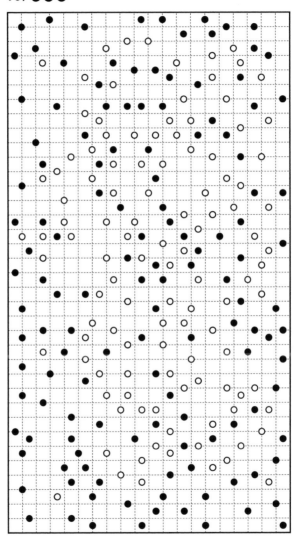

Shakashaka シャカシャカ

GUTEN, 2008

The challenge: Shade some cells with triangles so that all the remaining white areas are either squares or rectangles.

The rules: The shaded triangles take up half a cell and can be one of four orientations:

A number in a black cell indicates how many shaded triangles share a side with that cell. Cells may be left white. No square may be fully shaded.

How to solve it:

A. The starting grid.

B. **Freebies:** Start with the corners and the edges. The 2-cell in the corner and the 2-cell on the top edge have only two free sides each, which means that each cell adjacent to them must contain a shaded triangle. But which orientation of triangle? We need to refer to the Shakashaka battle-cry: 'Do not create acute angles!' We avoid acute angles (ones that are less than 90 degrees), since squares and rectangles do not have acute angles. For each of the cells adjacent to the 2-cell in the corner and the 2-cell on the top edge there is only one possible orientation of triangle, and I have shaded them in. All other orientations would have created an acute angle (i.e. a spiky bit) between a triangle and either the grid edge or the numbered cell. Likewise, a 3-cell on the edge of the grid has only three free sides, so every side must be used and, again, only one orientation is possible for the triangles in the two cells along

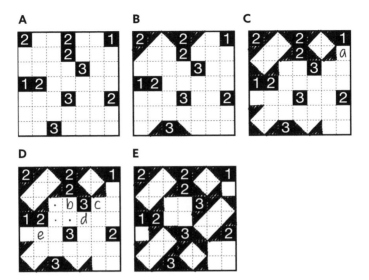

the edge, because all other orientations create an acute angle. We can shade in these two cells, and we'll determine the orientation of the third side later.

C. Now it's time to start thinking about the white squares and rectangles being created by the shaded triangles. The diagonal of every shaded triangle must ultimately be the outline of a white square or rectangle. So if that diagonal line hits an edge, or a numbered cell, we need to add a triangle that continues the outline at right angles. Keep turning corners where the cells force you to, either because a diagonal hits an edge, or because a numbered square requires it. For example, we know that **a** cannot have a triangle in it, because if it did the 1-cell above it would have two triangles, which is forbidden, and there is only one possible position for a triangle in the cell left of **a**.

D. Cell **b** must be empty, because the 2-cell above it already has its full tally of two triangles. This means that **c** and **d** adjacent to the 3-cell must each contain a triangle. The cells with dots must be empty, since there is no way you could put triangles in them to complete a square or rectangle – which in turn means that **e** must contain a triangle.

E. The finished grid.

➡ In 1704 the French priest and mathematician Sébastien Truchet published a short article about the interesting combinations of patterns that you can make using a single square tile split down the diagonal into two colors. A tile colored in this way is now called a 'Truchet tile' and its four orientations in a grid are precisely the four possible shaded cells of a Shakashaka puzzle. *Nikoli* reader Guten was unaware of Truchet tiles when he devised Shakashaka – the name is a derivation from *shakaku*, the Japanese for 'oblique angle' – but both Guten and Truchet seem to have been attracted by the striking aesthetics of triangles arranged in this way. As the only *Nikoli* puzzle that works with diagonals, Shakashaka puzzles have a distinctive look that breaks through the rigid orthogonality of the square grid. They are also charming to solve. As you fill in the grid you feel like you are an archaeologist excavating ancient ruins, slowly revealing the architectural footprints of previous civilizations. According to *Nikoli* staff, Shakashaka is especially popular among its young female readers, who find it *kawaii*, or cute. Boom! Shakashaka, Shakashaka the room. Tick, tick, tick, tick, boom!

1/ 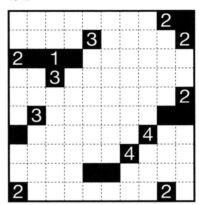 NOBUYUKI SAKAMOTO

2/ 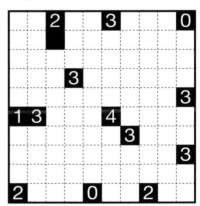 HAGA NODUKI

3 / 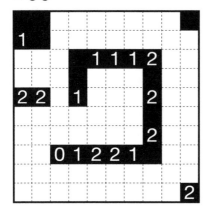 TENPO

4 / 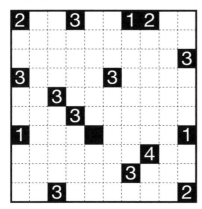 BUNSHI MOTOR

5/ 🥷🥷 HOTSUMITABA

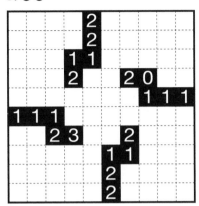

6/ 🥷🥷🥷 KATORYU

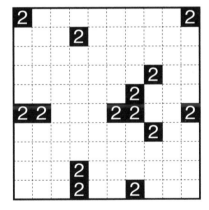

7/ MOMONGA

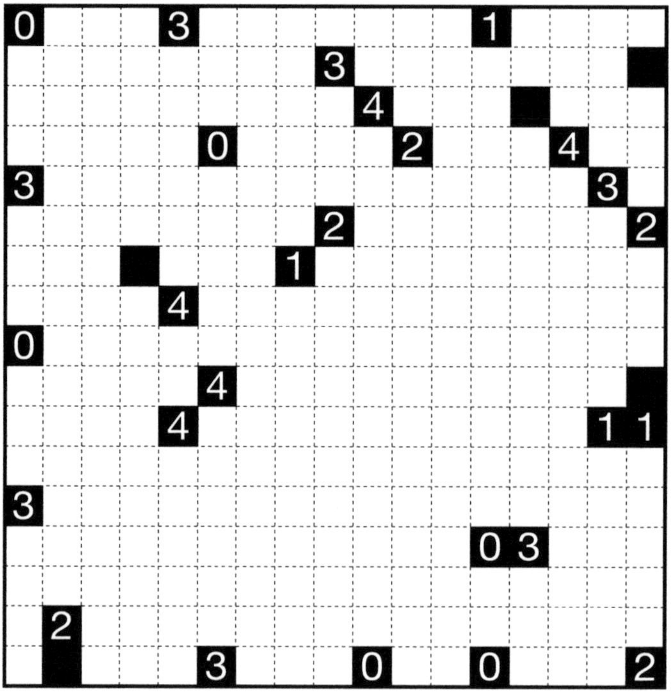

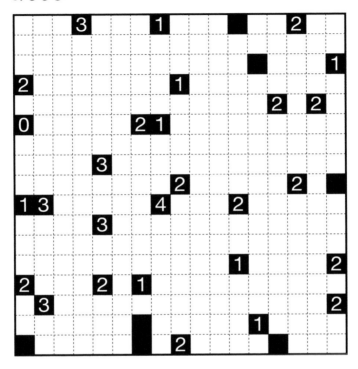

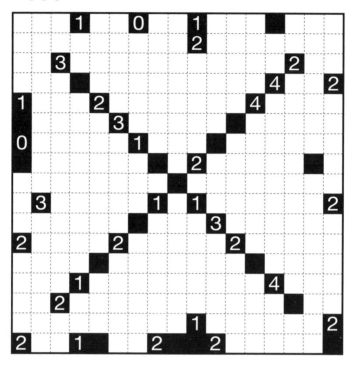

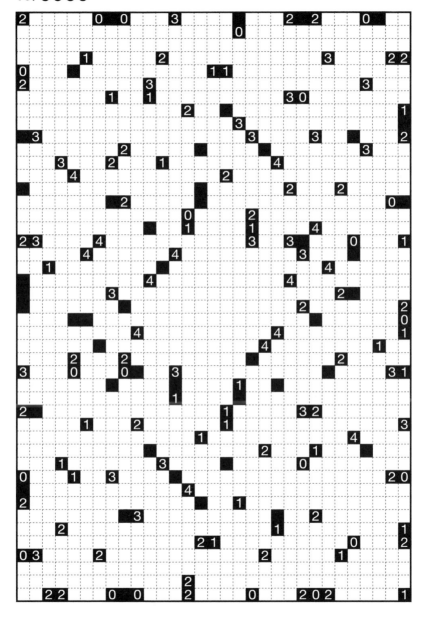

Herugolf ヘルゴルフ

ALKALI-KOJO-CHO, 2013

The challenge: Hit each ball into its own unique hole with shorter and shorter horizontal or vertical putts.

The rules: Each ball is a circle with a number in it. The holes are the cells with an H. The first putt travels the distance described by the number in the circle. Each successive putt travels one cell fewer than the putt before. Successive putts can be in the same direction, or can change direction. A ball must reach its hole at precisely the end of a putt, but not necessarily at the end of a 1-cell putt. Putts may not cross each other, nor share the same cells, nor go back on themselves. No two balls may go into the same hole. The shaded areas are bunkers. A putt can cross a bunker but cannot land on one.

How to solve it:

A. The starting grid.

B. The 3-ball in the top-left corner must move three cells in its first putt either horizontally or vertically. It cannot move vertically since it will land in a bunker, so it must move horizontally. Likewise, the 3-ball in the top-right corner must move three cells downwards, since if it moved three cells horizontally it would land in the cell now occupied by the first 3-ball. The remaining 3-ball has only one possible move – downwards – which blocks in the 2-ball in the bottom left, which must therefore move two upwards.

C. After moving three cells in their first putts, each 3-ball must now move two cells in their second. There is only one possible direction that each of these balls can move. Two of the balls reach their holes after this putt. The third ball still has its final

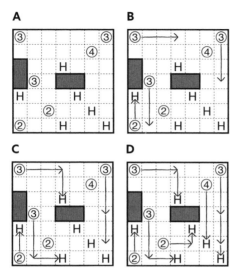

(one-cell) putt left, but it's not clear yet which is the correct hole.

D. The 4-ball in the second row can only go in one direction for its first move of four, and it holes in one. The ball in the right column therefore holes in the bottom-right corner, and the remaining 2-ball has only one possible path to the last hole.

➥ Herugolf was cooked up by the puzzle chemist known as Alkali-Kojo-Cho ('Alkali Factory Manager'). I was hoping that the name was a Japanese transliteration of 'Hell-golf' but, in fact, it comes from the word *heru*, meaning reduce, since each putt reduces in length by 1 cell. I love the humor in turning golf into a game of logic, and the playfulness of the grid designs.

1 / 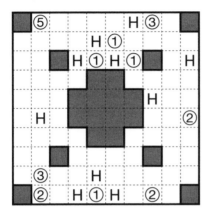 KOKIN

2 / COMMON TIME

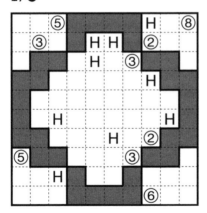

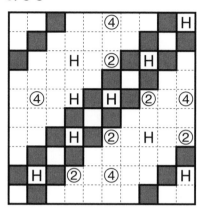

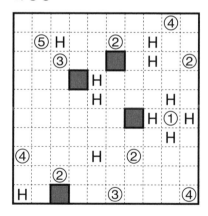

5 / 🥷🥷 KOKIN

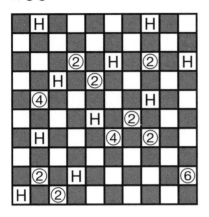

6 / 🥷🥷🥷 FOUR-VECTOR

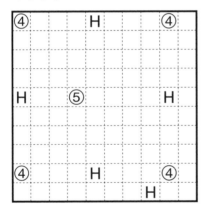

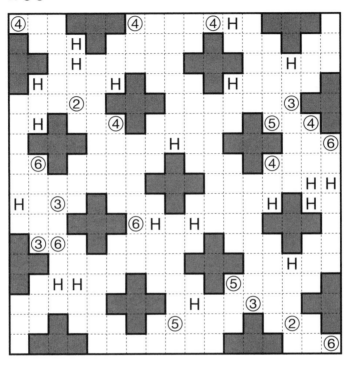

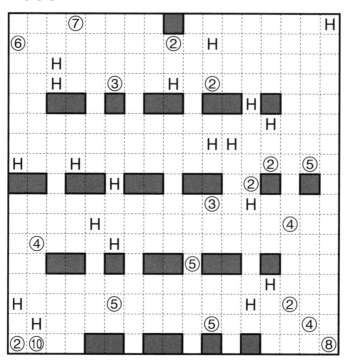

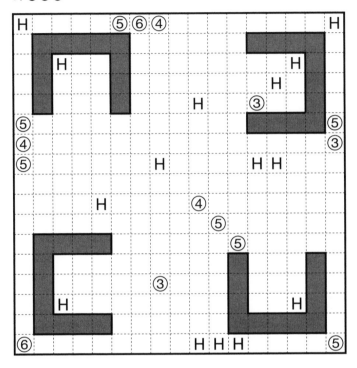

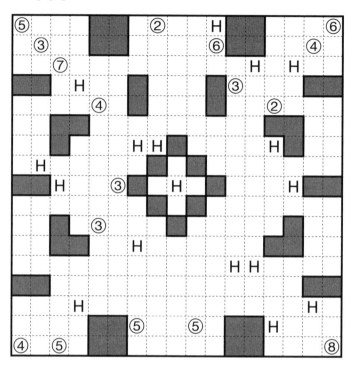

THE
PUZZLE
POET

A sign on the wall says the rules of puzzle class are:

1) No shouting out the answer.
2) Listen to the teacher's explanation.
3) Don't break the puzzles.

I'm in Torito, a puzzle shop in Akihabara, Tokyo's geeky neighborhood of cheap electronics stores, manga bookshops and cafés with waitresses dressed up as domestic maids. Torito sells hundreds of different types of puzzle, from metal disentanglement puzzles to wooden puzzle boxes to Rubik's Cubes, and also hosts afterschool puzzle classes for children. It seemed like an appropriate venue to meet Tetsuya Nishio.

Nishio, aged 62, is the puzzle master's puzzle master, an inventor, competitor, editor, mentor and the only person in the world whose name has become a Sudoku solving technique, the 'nishio'. (This is a strategy in which you make an assumption and see where it leads you. If you get a contradiction, you know the assumption was wrong.) He wears his white hair in a bob, which makes him look bohemian and approachable, despite his reputation as a fiendish tormentor of minds.

In the mid-1980s, the publishing house Sekai Bunka launched *Puzzler* magazine. It featured a section called 'Tough Puzzle Creation School', of which Nishio was the strict but benevolent headmaster. He held monthly contests for the best original puzzle, and also set puzzles that enabled readers to compete against each other. 'I recruited as apprentices those players who did well,' he says. He published harder puzzles than those in *Nikoli*, which made *Puzzler* especially popular with the brightest young puzzlists, and he became a father figure for a generation of solvers and creators.

As well as nurturing talent, however, Nishio also came up with many of his own ideas. He likes art, which he says is what inspired him to try to invent a puzzle that produced a picture when solved. His first attempts, he adds, were not satisfactory. 'They either failed to make detailed images or lacked a clean and fresh feel to them. Then, all of a sudden, the idea of O'Ekaki occurred to me. I tried it out. Voilà, it turned out to be one that satisfied my expectations.'

O'Ekaki means *Paint by numbers*. (Some solvers may wonder if the 't' isn't a typo.) It became the first Japanese logic puzzle to become an international success – a decade and a half before Sudoku – although bizarrely this had nothing to do with Nishio. The same puzzle concept was independently invented at the same time by Non Ishida, a Japanese graphic designer who had the idea after she won a competition to create a 'picture' on the side of a Tokyo skyscraper by turning lights on and off inside the building. A British puzzle designer saw her puzzles, called them Nonograms, and sold them to the *Sunday Telegraph*, who has published them continuously since 1990, where they are now known as Griddlers.

In Japan, Nishio was for many years the dominant personality in puzzledom, a prolific author of books and puzzles, as well as an expert solver. He was an early enthusiast of Number Place, as Sudoku was originally called and under which name it appeared in *Puzzler*. When the puzzle took off internationally he took part in the inaugural World Sudoku Championships in 2006, placing fourth, the highest finisher in the Japanese team. ('I don't think of myself as a puzzle ninja,' he says, laughing. 'Please describe me as a puzzle poet!') Killer Sudoku, a popular variant of Sudoku, was invented by one of Nishio's apprentices.

We talk about what makes a good puzzle. He thinks a puzzle should tell a story, based on logic, and that the solver should not have to do the same thing again and again. He adds that the best puzzles are well balanced between the 'part' and the 'whole'; in other words they require you, as you solve them, to alternate your attention between the individual step and the complete picture. He suggests that this sense of paying attention to details, but keeping an overall sense of balance, is a Japanese trait, evident for example in the art of cultivating bonsai miniature trees. In O'Ekaki, the switch of attention between the part and the whole is especially satisfying. The slow reveal of the picture is always tantalizing, and particularly addictive. Another element that makes the puzzle enjoyable is that you don't need a very large grid to be able to produce an image that is interesting and recognizable. The black-and-white cells in an O'Ekaki grid are analogous to the pixels in a black-and-white digital photograph.

Nishio's puzzle is now known around the world by many names, including Hanjie, Picross and Paint by Numbers. Perhaps its most high-profile moment came in 2015, when British spy agency GCHQ launched a Christmas puzzle challenge that is said to have attracted a million would-be solvers. The first part was an O'Ekaki grid which, when filled in, revealed a QR code for a website – which in turn contained the second part of the challenge.

O'Ekaki remains popular in Japan and, contrary to many things there, bigger is better when it comes to this puzzle. A recent book of 100 giant O'Ekaki problems sold 20,000 copies. It has fold-out pages with 180 x 70-cell grids, in other words 12,600 cells whose statuses need to be determined. If you tick off a cell every 10 seconds, which is good going, this puzzle will still take you 35 hours to complete!

Here I've chosen five of Nishio's hand-made puzzles that appeared in his book O'Ekaki Heaven.

O'Ekaki お絵かきロジック

1988

The challenge: Shade in cells to reveal a picture.

The rules: The numbers on the left and on the top represent the lengths of blocks of shaded cells in those rows and columns. The shaded cell blocks appear in the same order as the numbers. There is at least one blank cell between two shaded blocks.

How to solve it:

A. The starting grid.

B. Start by looking for numbers that are more than half the length of the grid, since these numbers will give us our first shaded cells. For example, one row and one column have a single 8. There are only three possible positions for each 8: starting on the first, second and third cells, as indicated by the arrows. Whichever position the 8-block is in it must cover the six middle cells, so we can shade them in.

C. The third column has blocks of 1 and 5. Remember the block of 1 has to come first (going from top to bottom). The block of 5 must include the cell that is already filled in, since if it were in the bottom five cells, the block would include the shaded cell and be 6 cells long. We can also deduce that the block of five can be no higher than the third row, since there must be at least two cells above it, one for the 1 block and one for a blank cell. The arrows show the limits of possible positions of the 5-block, and each of them includes the two lightly shaded cells, which we can fill in.

The eighth column has the blocks 2, 1, 2 and 1. By checking the possible positions of these blocks, we can deduce that the previously filled-in cell (5 cells down) must be the first block of 1. If it is any other of the blocks, there is not enough space.

A

Column clues:
```
                    2
                1 1 1
        1   4   1 1 2
      1 3 5 8 1 1 3 1 5 3
```
Row clues:
```
      3
1 1 2
  4 2
  2 2
    8
  3 2
  3 2
    5
    1
    4
```

B

Column clues:
```
                    2
                1 1 1
        1   4   1 1 2
      1 3 5 8 1 1 3 1 5 3
```
Row clues:
```
      3
1 1 2
  4 2
  2 2
    8
  3 2
  3 2
    5
    1
    4
```

C

Column clues:
```
                    2
                1 1 1
        1   4   1 1 2
      1 3 5 8 1 1 3 1 5 3
```
Row clues:
```
      3
1 1 2
  4 2
  2 2
    8
  3 2
  3 2
    5
    1
    4
```

D

Column clues:
```
                    2
                1 1 1
        1   4   1 1 2
      1 3 5 8 1 1 3 1 5 3
```
Row clues:
```
      3
1 1 2
  4 2
  2 2
    8
  3 2
  3 2
    5
    1
    4
```

And if it is the first block of 1, there is only one possible position for two blocks after it. The first block can be in two positions, as indicated by the arrows, so we can only fill in the cell that is the overlap of both these positions.

D. When solving O'Ekaki you must not only concentrate on the shaded cells, but also mark in the cells that must be empty. For example, the cell on the top row, five along, must be empty, and I have drawn an X there. We know it is empty, since this column starts with a 4-block, and if the 4-block started in the first row it would make a block of 5, since the fifth cell down is already filled in, which is forbidden. I've drawn an arrow to show the limit of how far upwards the 4-block could reach. Remember, the arrow is only showing how far the 4-block could reach, for

E

F

the purposes of crossing off squares that must be empty. The 4-block could also head downwards to the sixth, seventh and eighth row; as yet we don't know. All we know is that the only cell that must be empty in the fifth column is the top one. The arrows in the grid show the limits of other unfinished blocks, and beyond those arrows I have placed Xs, denoting a cell that is definitely empty. We can also add the 5-block to the eighth row, since the two shaded cells determine its exact position, and put Xs in all the other cells of that row.

E. Using the Xs we have just marked, we can deduce further empty cells and mark them with an X. For example, there is no way a 3-block will fit in the bottom of the last column, since only two cells are free. And there is no way a 5-block will fit in the bottom of the penultimate column, since again only two cells are free. These Xs now fix the position of the 4-block on the bottom row. This helps us to fix the 3-block in the seventh column. Now we can put Xs on all other cells on the second bottom row, which means we now know where the 8-block goes in the fourth column. We're cooking on gas! By repeating this process of eliminating some squares, and filling in others, we will eventually fill the grid.

F. The completed grid.

The joy of solving O'Ekaki is that you feel a bit like an artist, as well as a puzzle-solver. Like the caricature of the painter by his easel who briskly dabs around the canvas, my eye is always darting across the grid, looking for openings, shading a cell up here and then another one down there. Often my pencil is counting cells back and forth along rows or columns, these brisk horizontal or vertical movements like a draftsman sketching out the lines of a figure. Once the cells start to fill in the grid I will stare at it and scrunch my eyes to see if I can begin to make out the final image. Usually I can't, which adds to the joyous surprise, and relief, of the final cells. The cryptic titles are never any help at all!

What I also like about O'Ekaki is that it gets across the idea that often objects look totally different from one side as they do the other, even though how they look from one side is entirely dependent on how they look from the other. The interplay between the vertical and the horizontal clues is very hard to grasp intuitively, and can make for a tough puzzle. O'Ekaki can get crazily difficult. Not the ones here, though.

Here's an O'Ekaki tip that you might not be able to work out yourself. Once you have exhausted the basic strategies explained on the previous page, there may be a way to shade in cells or deduce they are empty by studying the edges of the grid, as I will show using the illustration overleaf of the top two rows of an O'Ekaki grid.

A. The gist of this tip is that if the very top, or very bottom, row contains a single block (or if the rightmost or leftmost column does), then you might be able to work out the position of this block by using the clues in the adjacent row (or column). For example, look at the illustration overleaf, in which the clue

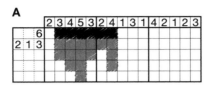

A

	2	3	4	5	3	2	4	1	3	1	4	2	1	2	3
6		■	■	■	■	■	■								
2 1 3															

B

	2	3	4	5	3	2	4	1	3	1	4	2	1	2	3
6	X	X	X	X				■	■	■				X	X
2 1 3								X		X					
									X						

C

	2	3	4	5	3	2	4	1	3	1	4	2	1	2	3
6	X	X	X	X	X								X	X	X
2 1 3	X	X	X	X	X	■	■	■	X	X	■	■	X	X	
								X		X					
								X		X					

for the top row is a 6, for a single 6-block. Let's suppose that this 6-block starts from the second cell, as I have marked in black. If the second cell is shaded, then from the 3-clue in the second column we must shade in the top three cells of the second column. Likewise, if the third cell on the top row is shaded, the 4-clue in the third column means we must shade in the top four cells of the third column. The image shows (in gray) all the cells we can shade from the vertical clues, and we see that once we have done this we have filled in a 6-block on the second row. But this 6-block on the second row contradicts the clues for the second row, which is 2-1-3. We can therefore deduce that the position of the 6-block on the top row is incorrect.

B.   What we are going to do now is the following: rather than use the clue for the top row to deduce the positions of shaded cells on the second row, we are going to look at the clue for the second row to deduce the positions of shaded cells on the top row. The second row has three blocks: a 2, then a 1, then a 3. Since between any two blocks there is at least one empty cell, we can deduce that the second row must contain a run of three cells that goes empty/shaded/empty, where the shaded cell is the 1-block. Our task is therefore to find a position for the 6-block on the top row that (once we have looked at the vertical clues) guarantees us a run on the second row of empty/shaded/empty. If a cell on the top row is shaded in, the only way to guarantee that the cell below it is empty is if the vertical clue is a 1. So, we need to look for a run of three vertical clues where the first and third are a 1 and the middle one is greater than 1: if the first-row cells are shaded in under these clues, we will get a run of empty/shaded/empty on the second row. There is only one run of three vertical clues where the first and third are a 1 and the middle one is greater than 1 (which are columns 8, 9 and 10), and so we know that the 6-block must cover these positions on the top row. I have shaded in these cells, with the vertical clues, and also arrows to show how far the 6-block could possibly go in either direction.

C. Using similar logic we can reduce by one cell in either direction how far the 6-block could go. For example, it can only extend as far as the 2 in the sixth column, because if it extended to the 3 in the fifth column, the second row would start with a 3-block, which is false. And it can only extend to the 2 in the twelfth column since if it went any further the second row would end with a 2-block, which is false. Whichever position the 6-block is in it must cover the five cells I have shaded. We can now determine every cell on the second row.

1/ 🥷 MINUS MAN

					1	1			1					2		1	1	
				3	1	1		5	1			2	4	3	1	6	5	5
				2	2	3	7	1	2	7	1	1	2	1	7	1	1	3
				2	3	4	4	3	5	3	1	3	1	1	2	4	1	1
		3	5															
1	1	2	1															
1	1	1	3															
	7	2	4															
1	2	4	4															
	4	2	3															
		4	5															
		2	5															
		3	2															
	4	1	4															
	1	1	1															
	5	2	1															
		8	3															
	7	1	3															
	4	3	1															

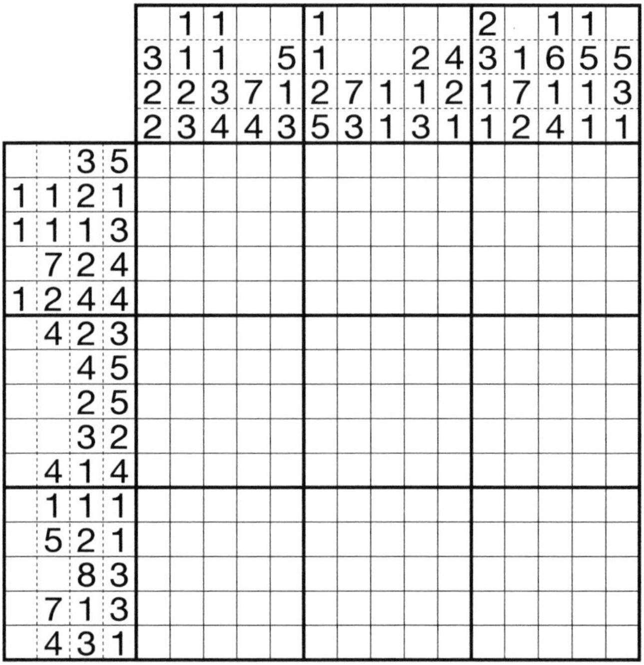

Nonogram puzzle.

Column clues (left to right, 15 columns):

						3						1		
	3				1	2		3		2	2			
	2	1	1	1	3	2	6	1	1	2	1	2	2	
3	7	2	7	8	5	2	1	5	4	2	1	1	4	5

Row clues (top to bottom, 15 rows):

3	3	
		10
3	3	
1	1	
1	6	
1	4	3
2	3	2
4	2	1
	3	2
		4
2	3	1
	2	8
3	3	2
3	2	2
	3	3

Column clues (top, read top-to-bottom per column):

```
            1 2       1 1     1
            3 2     1 2 2 1 7 1
            1 1 1 2 2 1 3 2 3 1   1   1
        4 6 4 2 1 2 5 2 1 2 3 2 3 3 1 2 1 2 2
      2 1 1 2 3 3 2 3 2 2 1 2 1 1 3 4 1 5 2 6
      6 2 2 3 4 1 3 2 4 4 3 1 2 5 6 2 4 3 5 3
```

Row clues (left):

```
                  15
              1  1  1
        3  1  1  1  1
              5  9  2
              5 11
              3  1  7
           1  5  1  1
           2  2  1  2
              1  2  2
           3  1  1  1
              4  3  1
           5  2  1  1
        1  1  1  2  1
              2  4  2
              4  4  7
           1  6  3  2
        1  2  2  4  4
     1  4  4  2  1  2
     5  1  2  3  1  1
        4  2  4  1  1
```

		2										4										
		1								5		1										
		3	1	2	2					1		2	1	5	6	7	3	2	4			
		1	1	1	1				2	2	1	2	1	1	5	3	2	2				
		2	2	1	4	6			2	2	1	3	1	1	1	1	3	2	1	2		
		3	3	5	3	1	2	2	13	2	1	3	1	1	1	1	3	2	1	2		
		1	1	1	1	7	1	7	2	1	1	2	6	5	5	5	6	2	1	2	5	

			4	1	5
5	1	7
1	1	1	8
1	2	1	5	1
1	1	1	6
2	1	1	1	5
1	2	1	1	3
3	1	1	1
1	3	1	6
2	1	3	1	1
2	11
1	1	2	2
5	2	2
5	1	1	5	2
5	1	7	1
1	1	7	1
1	1	10	1
7	1	5	2
2	2	4
4	1

5 / 😀😀😀 LAZYBONES!

Column clues (top of grid, columns 1–20, read top to bottom):

1	2	3	4	5	6	7	8	9	10	11	12	13	14	15	16	17	18	19	20
				1															
				2	2														
	4	5	1	1	3		1												
3	1	3	8	2	2	1	2	6					1						
4	2	2	3	1	2	3	12	6		1	2	2	11	4	1	2			
3	7	2	3	2	1	2	1	1	1	1	1	2	1	2	2	3	10	4	4

Row clues (left of grid, rows 1–20, top to bottom):

1. 2 4
2. 5 2
3. 6 4
4. 9 2
5. 8 5
6. 1 3 2 2
7. 1 2 3 2
8. 8 3 3
9. 2 2 2 3 3
10. 1 2 1 2 3
11. 1 1 1 1 1 1
12. 1 2 1 1 1 1
13. 1 2 2 2 1
14. 1 1 1 3 1
15. 2 2 2 1 2
16. 2 2 1
17. 1 2
18. 2 2
19. 3 3
20. 7

THE
WARRIOR
MONK

At the turn of the century a twenty-year-old student from Nagoya began inventing pencil-and-paper logic puzzles and putting them on his website. Naoki Inaba worked on his hobby three to four hours a day. He created a new type of puzzle each week. Only after three years of silence did anyone get in touch to say they had tried to solve one. It made no difference to Inaba's output: he continued with the same level of dedication, intensity and creativity for about a decade, at the end of which he had designed more than 400 unique types of logic puzzle. Inaba is by far the most prolific and brilliant inventor of logic puzzles of modern times.

'We think Naoki Inaba is the number-one puzzle creator in Japan, and in the world also. He is a kind of genius,' says Naoto Nagata, his editor at Gakken publishers.

Like all the puzzle masters of his generation, Inaba grew up reading *Nikoli* and *Puzzler* magazines. He submitted his first puzzle to *Puzzler* aged 16; it won the competition for puzzle of the month. Tetsuya Nishio, who we met in the previous chapter, phoned Inaba to congratulate him – early recognition for the teenager from the reigning puzzle king.

Inaba's puzzles have very simple rules. More so even than *Nikoli*'s puzzles, which often require a few lines of clarification of what's permissible and what isn't. The rules of an Inaba puzzle can usually be summarized in a single sentence. 'If I can't make a puzzle with a simple rule, I quit that puzzle,' he says.

Inaba's puzzles have a very different feel from *Nikoli*'s. Since he composed his puzzles with zero feedback, in many cases he only created a handful of examples before he moved on to the next one. He does not have a library of examples that provide a smooth learning curve as you progress through the difficulty levels. Even the easiest of his examples often require deep thought. Sometimes the hardest move is the first one.

I like this, though. Inaba says the harder 'jump-in' level at the beginning is deliberate. 'When coming up with a new puzzle, I enjoy the time when I have to think of the strategy of how to solve it, and I want the solver to enjoy that time also,' he says.

Inaba, now aged 37, studied physics, engineering and computer science at university. He initially wanted to become a puzzle programmer, and developed his own Sudoku generator, which is still his cash cow. A Sudoku magazine he compiles sells 70,000 copies every two months, which he estimates makes up about 10 per cent of the sales of all Japanese Sudoku publications. After briefly working for a software company, he started to collaborate with a Tokyo grammar school to develop educational puzzles and toys.

He invents many puzzles – not just logic-grid ones – such as Menseki Meiro ('Area Maze'), which requires solvers to find side lengths or areas of overlapping shapes. A book of Menseki Meiro was a bestseller in Japan.

For Inaba, coming up with ideas for new puzzles is easy – he just sits down at his desk and something pops into his head. He takes much longer to make actual examples of the puzzles, which he does by hand, drawing grids in a notebook. 'I'm very concerned with how my puzzles look,' he says. Sometimes he makes grids look symmetrical, placing their given elements in a geometrical pattern. At other times, he prefers asymmetry. In the Japanese *ikebana* tradition of flower arranging, asymmetry is thought to give compositions a more natural, less stagnant feel. Inaba echoes this sentiment: 'I want my puzzles to look beautiful. I want to make them look alive.'

He thinks he has maybe a thousand grid puzzles in him, so, with about 400 in the bag so far, he is not even halfway there. I've selected eight types that I really enjoy.

L-Panel エルパネル

2011

The challenge: Draw along the dotted lines to make L-shaped tiles, like the one below, made up of four cells each.

How to solve it:

A. The starting grid.
B. There is only one position for an L-tile that covers the top-left cell, so mark it in. The position of the other two L-shapes is now obvious.
C. The completed grid.

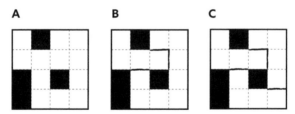

➡ Inaba has devised many puzzles that require tiling shapes into a grid, and in my opinion L-Panel, with only a single shape, distills this genre into its purest form. True to his reputation as a master of the simple rule, the challenge here is so easy to understand it barely needs stating. (It took me only nineteen words.) The first few examples are also a soft entry into Inaba's world. The larger ones, however, do require thought.

1 /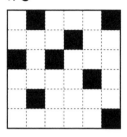

2 /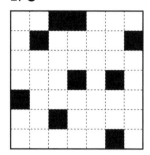

3 /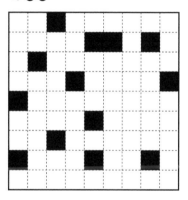

4 /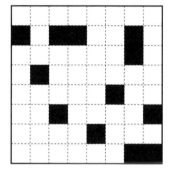

5 /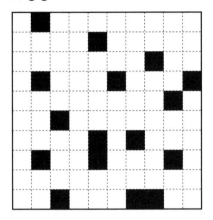

6 /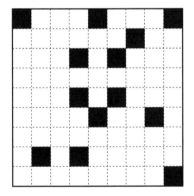

7/ 🥷🥷🥷

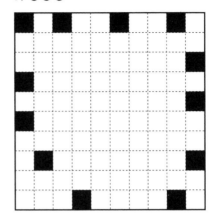

8/ 🥷🥷🥷

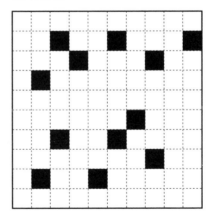

Marupeke ○×プレース

2009

The challenge: Fill in each empty cell with either an O or an X, so that no more than two consecutive cells, either horizontally, vertically or diagonally, contain the same symbol.

How to solve it:

A. The starting grid.
B. The cell between the two Os must contain an X, otherwise there is a diagonal run of three Os, which is forbidden.
C. The cell between the Xs on the third row must contain an O, otherwise there is a horizontal run of three Xs, which again is forbidden.
D. The cell on the bottom row beneath the Os in the second column must contain an X, otherwise there is a vertical run of three Os. Now you're on a roll. This new X threatens a diagonal run of three Xs, so there must be an O in the final cell of the second row. Continue using these strategies to complete the grid.
E. The completed grid.

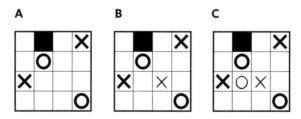

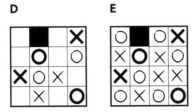

D

E

➥ 'This puzzle is like a simple equation,' says Inaba. 'In a simple equation two things lead to a third.' In other words, when you add, subtract, multiply or divide two numbers, you get a third number. 'I wanted to express this idea as simply as possible.' Marupeke - the name comes from *maru*, the word for circle, and *peke*, the word for X - is trickier than it looks. At first, solving the puzzle is a question of looking for two identical symbols in a row, or where they are separated by a space. But in the more complicated ones you need to think a few moves ahead, to make sure you don't create a situation in which two consecutive Xs and two consecutive Os lead to the same empty space. You'll never look at noughts and crosses the same way again!

1/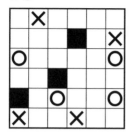

2/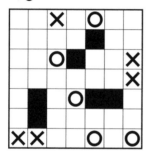

3/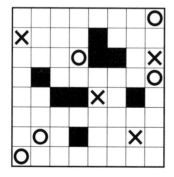

4 /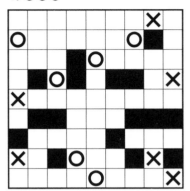

5 /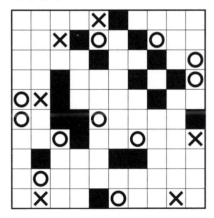

Block Number ナンバーブロック

1996

The challenge: The grid is divided into blocks. Fill each block with the number(s) starting from 1 and counting upwards. So a single-cell block contains just a 1. A two-cell block contains 1 and 2. A three-cell block contains 1, 2 and 3; and so on.

The rules: Cells containing numbers that are the same cannot be horizontally, vertically or diagonally adjacent.

How to solve it:

A. The starting grid.

B. Let's start with the cell I've marked **a**. It must be a 2, a 3 or a 4, since the block has four cells and 1 is already accounted for. Now consider the block above **a**: it has three cells, so they must contain a 1, a 2 and a 3. Since **a** is adjacent either vertically or diagonally to every cell in the block above it, it will be adjacent to a 2 and a 3, which means that **a** cannot be 2 or 3. So **a** is 4. Now look at the cell containing a 2. The only possible positions for the 2 in the block above it are each marked with a dot, which means that the only possible positions for the 2 in the top block are the cells marked with a cross. We can therefore deduce that **b** is not a 2, since **b** is adjacent to both crosses. So **c** must be 2 and **b** is 3.

C. The cell marked **d** shares a border with a 1, 2, 3 and a 4, and therefore cannot be a 1, 2, 3 or a 4. It is in a block of five cells, so it must be one of the digits from 1 to 5. We can therefore deduce **d** is 5. The cell marked **e** is the only one in its block that is not adjacent to a 3, so it must be the 3.

D. Now that the 3 is in place on the top row, we can deduce that cell **f** must also be a 3. Using similar reasoning **g** must be a 3

A

1			2

B

x	x		.
b	a	.	.
C			
1			2

C

		e	
3	4		
2	d		
1			2

D

		3	
3	4		
2	5	f	
1	9		2

E

		3	h
3	4		i
2	5	1	3
1	3	4	2

F

2	1	3	1
3	4	2	4
2	5	1	3
1	3	4	2

too. The cell adjacent to **g** must be a 4: we know this block has a 4 and it cannot be in the other remaining cell, which is diagonally adjacent to another 4. The last cell in this block must be a 1.

E. With a 1 now positioned in the bottom 5-block, we know that **h** must also be a 1, which means that **i** has to be 4. The remaining cell in this block is 2, and the remaining two cells in the top row fall into place.

F. The completed grid.

➡ Inaba invented this puzzle while still at secondary school. It involves relatively sophisticated solving strategies from the start – there are rarely any freebies with Naoki Inaba! What transfixes me with this puzzle is the emptiness of the opening grids. At first glance there seem to be too few clues to fill it all in. Yet, of course, the arrangement does determine a unique answer – and one that can be worked out through logical steps – making progression through the puzzle a thrilling experience.

In the UK this puzzle is also known as Suguru, a word chosen by British company Puzzler Media, which felt that the words 'number' and 'block' didn't 'sufficiently reflect the qualities' of the puzzle. Suguru, a Japanese boy's name which roughly translates as 'number group', does. Personally, I quite like the unintended meanings of the literal translation. When solving these puzzles, you will face mental blocks. And if you get really stuck, go walk round the block. You'll feel much better for it.

1/😈😈

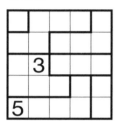

2/😈😈

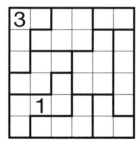

3 / 🥷🥷🥷

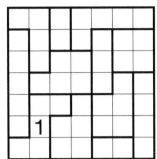

4 / 🥷🥷🥷

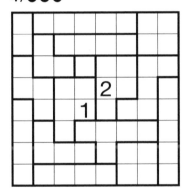

Straight Cross ストレートクロス

2011

The challenge: Fill the cells with numbers from 1 to 9 so that each horizontal and vertical strip contains consecutive numbers.

The rules: A strip is made up of the adjacent white cells between edges of the grid and/or black squares. The numbers must be consecutive but not necessarily in numerical order, nor must the sequence start with 1. So, if the digits are 2, 3 and 4, for example, they could be in the order 2-3-4, 2-4-3, 3-2-4, 3-4-2, 4-2-3 or 4-3-2.

How to solve it:

A. The starting grid.
B. The top row contains a 1 and a 4, so we can deduce that the other two cells must be a 2 and a 3. The cell marked **a** cannot be a 2, since the vertical strip from **a** already contains a 2. So **a** must be 3, and the final cell of the top row is 2. The cell marked **b** is part of a vertical strip including a 1, which means it must contain a 2 or a 3. It is also part of a horizontal strip containing a 2 and a 5, which means it must be a 3 or a 4. So **b** can only be a 3, which means that the cell above it is a 2 and the other empty cell in **b**'s row is a 4. Note that unlike Sudoku it is possible for two digits to appear in the same row or column if they are separated by a shaded cell.
C. Cell **c** is part of a horizontal strip with a 2, so it contains either 1 or 3. But it can't be 3, since it is also part of a vertical strip that already has a 3. So **c** is 1. With a 1, 2 and 3 in that vertical strip the only contender for **d** is 4.
D. The final column must have a 3 and a 4 and each can fit in only one position. That leaves us with a single cell for the 5.
E. The completed grid.

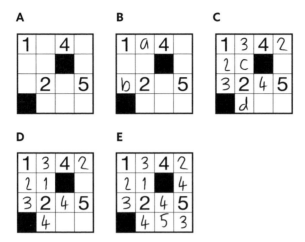

A

1		4	
		■	
	2		5
■			

B

1	*a*	4	
		■	
b	2		5
■			

C

1	3	4	2
2	*c*	■	
3	2	4	5
■	*d*		

D

1	3	4	2
2	1	■	
3	2	4	5
■	4		

E

1	3	4	2
2	1	■	4
3	2	4	5
■	4	5	3

➡ 'The idea behind Straight Cross was to combine Sudoku and the crossword,' says Inaba. I find this puzzle more rewarding than Sudoku because you have to take into account the numerical value of the number, which adds an unusual twist. It is nice to be thinking in terms of maximums and minimums, by which I mean the highest and lowest values these strips can contain, and how these values fit in with the other strips. I like the hopping from horizontal to vertical thinking too. Short strips are our friends since they limit the length of the run. Inaba chose the word 'straight' for the title because in poker a straight means a run of consecutive cards. He chose the word 'cross' because the hard ones will make you so upset you will cry. (Not really.)

1 / 🥷🥷

```
■     7   ■
  3 ■   3
■ 2
  4 ■
1 ■   5
■ 4   ■
```

2 / 🥷🥷

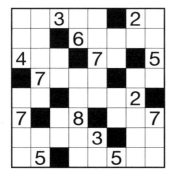

```
  2 ■
5 ■   4
■   3 ■ 7
6 ■ 7
7 ■ 3 ■
3 ■ 4
■ 6
```

3 / 🥷🥷🥷

```
  3 ■ 2
■ 6
4 ■ 7 ■ 5
■ 7 ■
■ 2 ■
7 ■ 8 ■ 7
3 ■
5 ■ 5
```

142

4 /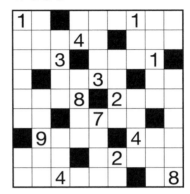

5 /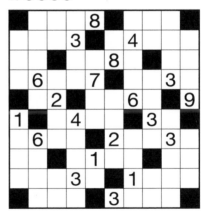

Walls ウォールズ

2009

The challenge: Fill each empty cell with either a vertical or a horizontal line, so that the number in each black cell equals the combined length of the lines ending at that cell. Lines cannot go through black cells.

How to solve it:

A. The starting grid.

B. The five cells marked **a**, **b**, **c**, **d** and **e** are the only cells that can contain horizontal or vertical lines that may potentially end at the 4-cell. Since we know that the total length of lines ending at the 4-cell is 4, we can deduce that the lines *must* pass through **b** and **d**. If a line didn't pass through **b**, or through **d**, then the total possible length of lines ending at the 4-cell would be 3. So in **b** and **d** we can mark in lines that end at the 4-cell.

C. A vertical line in **a** would mean that a line of length 2 ends in a 1-cell, which is not permitted. So **a** must contain a horizontal line, from which we can deduce that **c** and **e** must contain horizontal lines that eventually end at the 4-cell.

D. Now let's consider the 3-cell. For lines of total length 3 to end at the 3-cell, **f** must be a horizontal line – if it wasn't the total possible length of lines ending at the 3-cell would only be 2. Once we fill in **f**, all the other empty cells fall into line. A horizontal line of 2 is now coming from the 2-cell, so the cells above and below it must be horizontal. So the 1-cell in the top row has a line connected to it on the left side, which means the cell to its right must have a vertical line; and so on.

E. The completed grid.

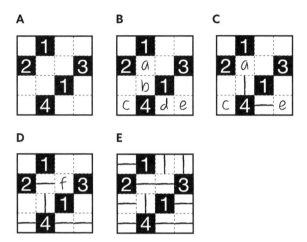

➡ Walls is my favorite Inaba puzzle. It is a perfect piece of puzzle minimalism. No shading, no symbols. Just horizontal and vertical lines. The rule is incredibly simple but solving the puzzle can be spectacularly difficult – before long you'll feel like banging your head against a brick wall. You have to work out quite a few strategies to solve this puzzle, but don't be daunted by the steep learning curve. Walls is a beautiful puzzle. The organic, tiled look of the completed grid displays a naturalness that hides its cruelty. Here are some tips: look at cells with a small number. Obviously a 0-cell means you can fill in the four cells adjacent to it: horizontal above and below; vertical on the left and right. But a 1-cell can also be a good place to start – again, once you know which cell connects to it, you can fill in its other neighbors. Big numbers that look a bit blocked in can also be helpful – maybe the restrictions on where the lines can go will give you a clue. Sometimes you need to suppose what would happen if you placed a line in a certain cell, then work out how the grid starts to fill in and see how it might lead to a contradiction. If it does, you know you can draw the other type of line in the original cell.

1 /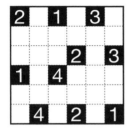

2 /

3 /

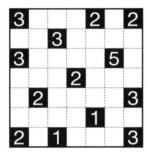

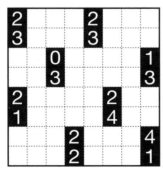

146

4 /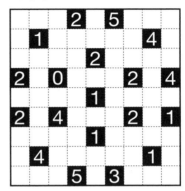

5 /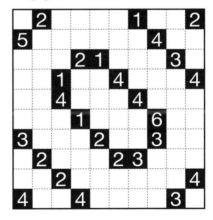

6/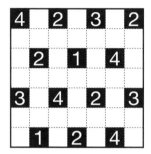

7/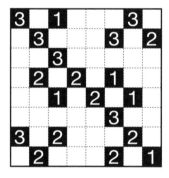

8 /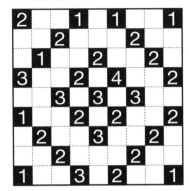

9 /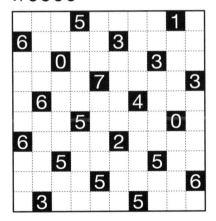

Searchlights ブライトライト

2011

The challenge: Place searchlights (circles) in some cells of the grid.

The rules: A number in a black cell indicates how many lights you would see from that cell looking horizontally and vertically (but not diagonally). You can see through lights but not through black cells. A cell can have at most one light.

How to solve it:

A. The starting grid.

B. There are five possible positions for the four lights that are visible from the 4-cell, which I have marked **a**, **b**, **c**, **d** and **e**. We know that **b** and **c** cannot *both* contain lights, since they are also both visible from the 1-cell, which must have only a single light in its line of sight. The four lights visible from the 4-cell are therefore **a**, **d**, **e** and *either* **b** or **c**. Since the light that is visible from the 1-cell is either **b** or **c**, we know that all the other positions visible from the 1-cell have no lights in them, so we can mark them with dots as a memory aid.

C. The 2-cell in the top left has only one available position for its second light, which is the final cell in the top row. Likewise, there are only two possible positions for the two lights visible from the other 2-cell in the first column, which determines which light is visible from the 1-cell (and the final light visible from the 4-cell).

D. The completed grid.

A

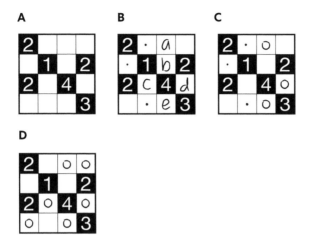

B

C

D

→ Between 1990 and 2012, Microsoft included a solitaire logic game as part of its Windows operating system. Minesweeper consisted of a grid of cells, some of which were blank and some of which contained numbers denoting how many mines were hidden in adjacent squares. Inaba compares Searchlights to Minesweeper. 'The essence is the same but [my puzzle] is a simplification, and better,' he says.

If you liked Walls you'll also enjoy Searchlights, since they require similar solving strategies. The feel is very different, though: rather than blocking off cells with walls, you are lighting up corridors. The puzzle, however, can be very tricky to start. Like chess, you often need to be working many moves ahead. But once you have cracked the beginning, it does get easier.

The most useful squares to start with tend to be the biggest numbers, since they may force some deductions, as the 4-cell did in the example. A 1-cell can be helpful too, since if you know which direction its light is coming from you can eliminate all the cells in all the other directions. Always remember that lights do not shine through black cells, but they do shine through other lights.

1/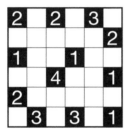

2/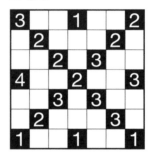

3/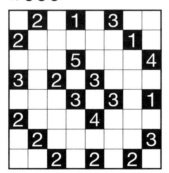

4 /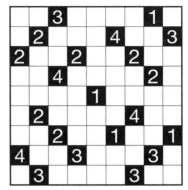

5 /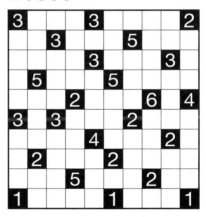

Ren-Katsu 連カツ

2010

The challenge: Divide the grid into regions made up of cells connected horizontally or vertically, so that each region contains a sequence of numbers that increases consecutively from 1 (so every region must contain a 1, and sometimes contains only a 1).

How to solve it:

A. The starting grid.

B. Since all regions contain a sequence of numbers that increase consecutively, no region can contain the same number twice. So we can draw a line between any two adjacent cells with the same number.

C. The region containing the 3 in the bottom-right corner must also contain the 2 to its left, and also the 1 above the 2, otherwise the 2 and the 3 would be cut off in their own region, and every region must include a 1. No region can contain the same number twice, so we can conclude that this region must stop here, since the only way to expand it would mean incorporating one of the 3s adjacent to the 1. By closing off this region, we also close a second region above it. On the bottom left of the grid we can extend the line between the 2s by a cell, otherwise we would have a region containing a single 2, which is forbidden.

D. We can close the region in the top row by enclosing the adjacent 1 and the 2, since there is no way to extend the region to include a 3 without incorporating another 1. The 1 in the top corner cannot reach a 2 without incorporating another 1, so it must be in its own region. There is now only one way to finish the boundary for the final two regions.

E. The completed grid.

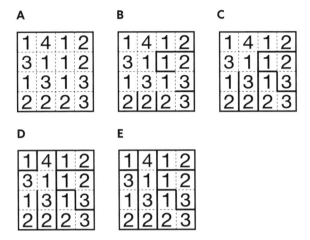

A

1	4	1	2
3	1	1	2
1	3	1	3
2	2	2	3

B

1	4	1	2
3	1	1	2
1	3	1	3
2	2	2	3

C

1	4	1	2
3	1	1	2
1	3	1	3
2	2	2	3

D

1	4	1	2
3	1	1	2
1	3	1	3
2	2	2	3

E

1	4	1	2
3	1	1	2
1	3	1	3
2	2	2	3

➥ In 2007 Inaba met his wife, Natsumi, who was a contestant in a puzzle championship. She now works as his manager and is the first reader of his puzzles. One of her favorites is Ren-Katsu, which Inaba invented for the Japanese Puzzle Championship. The name is an abbreviation of the words *renban*, meaning consecutive numbers, and *bunkatsu*, meaning division. If, however, you put the Japanese characters into Google Translate, the phrase that comes out is 'knit cutlet'. Brain cutlet, more like. Ren-Katsu is not a puzzle for beginners. Perhaps no other puzzle in this book combines so well the pleasure of such a simple challenge with the pain of trying to solve it.

1 / 🍙

4	4	4	1	4	2
1	2	3	5	3	5
3	2	1	3	1	2
1	5	6	2	6	5
4	2	3	1	4	1
6	1	3	2	3	2

2 / 🍙🍙

2	5	2	4	5	1	2
3	5	3	4	1	2	1
2	1	4	2	2	6	3
1	6	3	4	3	5	1
5	4	5	1	2	3	2
1	2	3	6	1	3	1
4	1	5	4	1	4	2

3 / 🍙🍙

2	2	5	1	5	1	3	1
1	3	6	3	6	2	4	6
3	2	4	1	4	1	2	1
4	3	5	6	1	5	1	5
1	2	1	3	4	1	4	1
6	5	4	2	3	2	3	6
1	6	5	4	5	1	5	1
4	2	3	1	6	1	6	1

4 / 🥷🥷🥷

1	2	3	4	5	6	7	8	9
2	4	2	3	4	5	6	7	6
4	5	1	2	1	2	8	1	7
5	3	1	1	2	1	4	6	8
6	5	5	6	6	4	2	9	2
3	3	5	6	9	3	1	3	4
3	2	1	7	8	1	3	4	5
2	1	2	3	3	2	5	2	1
1	4	4	3	3	1	2	5	3

5 / 🥷🥷🥷

8	2	4	2	6	3	2	5	1	3
1	5	6	1	2	1	7	4	2	1
7	3	1	3	5	2	6	1	3	4
4	5	3	6	1	4	3	2	7	5
1	3	4	2	9	9	4	5	8	3
7	1	2	3	9	9	2	4	6	4
4	5	3	4	6	5	4	6	1	3
5	2	1	5	4	2	3	1	3	2
6	1	2	7	2	3	1	6	7	1
8	5	7	4	3	1	2	8	5	4

Stones ストーンズ

2009

The challenge: The grid is divided into blocks by thick lines. Place stones in cells so that the statements in each of the blocks are correct.

The rules: A block with an equals sign (=) will need to have an equal number of stones either side of the sign. A block with a 'greater than' sign (>) will need to have more stones on one of the sides than the other, and so on. A number alongside a row or column indicates the number of stones that must appear in that row or column. A cell without a symbol either contains a single stone, or is empty.

How to solve it:

A. The starting grid.

B. The 3 next to the bottom row means that the bottom row contains three stones. There are four possible places for the stones, so three of them will have a stone and one of the cells will be empty. We can deduce that the third cell along cannot have a stone, so it must be the empty one. Imagine, for example, if the third cell did contain a stone. It would be in a block with a 'greater than' symbol, which tells us that the cell on the other side of the symbol must have more stones than the cell with a single stone. But a cell cannot have more than a single stone in it, so we end up with a contradiction. Once we have deduced that the third cell along the bottom line is empty, we must place a stone in the other free cell in its block, in order for the statement in that block to make sense; it thus reads 'one stone is greater than no stones', which is correct.

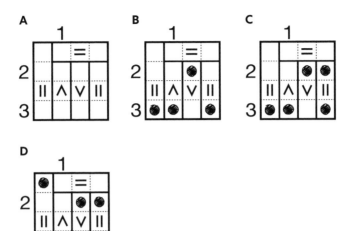

C. For the block in the final column to make sense we need to put a stone on the other side of the equals sign. This stone brings the number of stones in the second row to 2, which is exactly the number indicated at the side of the grid. Since the second row can have no more stones, to make the block in the first column mathematically correct, we need to place a stone in the top-left corner cell.

D. The completed grid.

Inaba suggested I include Stones because his wife Natsumi made important suggestions when he was devising it. The puzzle involves different strategies from the other ones in this book because it is the only one that uses inequalities. In problems 3 and 4, the ≤ and ≥ signs mean 'less than or equal to' and 'more than or equal to'.

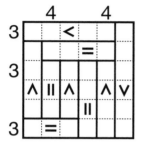

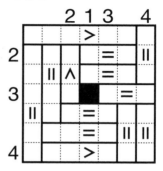

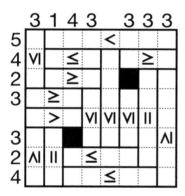

160

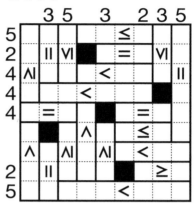

4 / 🍎🍎🍎

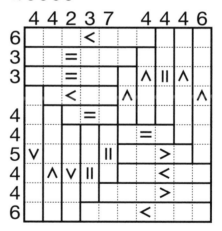

5 / 🍎🍎🍎🍎

THE
SUPER
SENSEI

Rarely can someone have discovered their calling so serendip-itously. Tetsuya Miyamoto came from a poor family in Osaka. He hated school and dropped out. Inspired by *Star Trek*, or more specifically a desire to be like Spock, he applied to study astronomy at university. He failed twice to get in and ended up studying drama. He became a teacher at a grammar school out of necessity; as a drama graduate it was the highest-paying job he could find. But Miyamoto loved it, and soon teaching primary-school mathematics became his overriding obsession. He has now published almost 200 books, with combined sales in Japan of about three million copies. Mostly they are puzzle-based workbooks for kids, but he has also written a bestselling summary of his classroom philosophy: *The Art of Teaching Without Teaching.*

The Miyamoto method is that you do not teach primary-level children how to do mathematics. 'You only need to give them very interesting puzzles,' he says. If the problems are interesting, they will want to solve them, and learn by themselves, each at his or her own speed. 'No child should be forced to do anything,' he adds. 'You need to accept that they are who they are.' He is dismissive of any pedagogical technique that emphasises rote learning or memorization, which is quite a radical statement in Japan. 'Enjoy the trial and error, and the answer will come to you. The essence of mathematics is *keep thinking*.'

Miyamoto's commitment to his job is almost comically intense. He used to get up at 2 a.m. to prepare that day's classes. However, since he got married for the first time in 2016, aged 56, he allows himself a sleep-in and wakes at 4 a.m. He writes all his own material, and this is how, in 2004, he found himself trying to create an entertaining puzzle for his Year 3 pupils that used addition, subtraction, multiplication and division.

He was an avid reader of both *Nikoli* and *Puzzler* magazines but considered their puzzles too difficult for eight-year-olds and not arithmetical enough for his students. So he invented the *kashikoku naru* puzzle, or 'the puzzle that makes you smarter'. His pupils enjoyed his creation – in fact, he says they became so engrossed by it that in the class he held on the day after an earthquake they did not even notice the large aftershocks. Gradually the puzzle spread from his Tokyo classroom to the Japanese public. He has written about forty *kashikoku naru* books and has a fortnightly column in the *Yomiuri Shimbun*, the world's highest-circulation newspaper. His publisher came up with the name KenKen for the export market, from the word *ken*, which means 'wisdom'. KenKen thus translates as 'wisdom wisdom', or 'wisdom squared', which I prefer since it is less repetitive and more on-brand. Of all the puzzles in this book, KenKen has had the most success in the West. It appears daily in the London *Times*, the *New York Times* and many other newspapers, and there's an annual tournament in the US.

Miyamoto's classroom is on the second floor of a small commercial building across from a rail line in central Tokyo. He now gives classes only on weekends, since many of his students live several hours away by train, and they wouldn't be able to get there on a school day. Even though his lessons are long – an hour and a half for eight-year-olds and two and a half hours for nine- to eleven-year-olds – he does not allow breaks. He claims his students neither get bored nor lose their concentration. Boring, he says, is being told that, say, 7 + 8 = 15. 'This is no fun. It doesn't cultivate your mind other than just memorizing the answer.' On the other hand, give a student a puzzle like KenKen, he says, and you never need to tell them if they are wrong or right. If they get to the end and the numbers don't fit, they know by themselves they have made a mistake, and they will look back at what they have done. 'They notice their own calculation mistakes. *This* is fun.'

In this way, he adds, puzzles teach students to be extremely careful when they calculate, as well as nurturing problem-solving skills. 'My students become smarter without even knowing it because they are indulged, and focused on solving fun and interesting problems. It raises their self-esteem every time they've completed a puzzle. And the starting point doesn't matter. They train themselves to keep challenging, never giving up.' Mathematical puzzles improve your maths, of course. But for Miyamoto what is more important is that they improve you as a human being: 'The focus, the perseverance, the spirit of never giving up. [My method] is basic training for living a better life.'

I first met Miyamoto at his classroom around noon. We hadn't finished talking by the time he had to leave for another appointment, so he suggested we continue over dinner, at the characteristically early time of 4.30 p.m. Miyamoto and his wife Wakaba eat one meal a day, in the late afternoon, which means no working time is lost when other people are eating breakfast or lunch. It also means mealtimes can be extravagant feasts, which our early dinner of sashimi, tempura, beef tongue, sake and shochu certainly was.

Miyamoto is neither a mathematician nor a computer programmer, and he makes all his KenKen by hand. 'The computer has no heart. But I am always thinking about entertaining my readers,' he says. Wakaba adds: 'People say his problems speak to them. They say they can imagine what he is thinking, and how he can bring them to the solution.' Miyamoto starts composing his puzzles by finding an interesting pattern in the completed grid and working backwards. 'The first puzzle I was addicted to was Sudoku. But I got tired of it after one month. I've now been making and solving KenKen for thirteen years and I am still not bored of making or solving it.'

KenKen 賢くなるパズル

TETSUYA MIYAMOTO, 2004

The challenge: Fill the grid with numbers, so that each number appears only once in every row and column.

The rules: The numbers used are 1 up to the number of cells in each row or column. So if there are four cells you'll use the numbers 1 to 4; if there are six cells you'll use 1 to 6; and so on. The grid is divided into 'cages', each containing a target number in its top left corner. Using only one arithmetical operation in each case – addition, subtraction, multiplication or division – you must produce the target number using all the numbers in that cage.

How to solve it:

A. The starting grid.
B. The grid is 3 cells by 3 cells, so it will contain only the numbers 1, 2 and 3, each of which will appear only once in any row or column. An important insight in solving KenKen is the realization that numbers can appear more than once in a cage, so long as the rule about only appearing once in any row or column is not broken. Look at the 18-cage. The only way for a combination of three digits made up from either 1, 2 or 3 to produce 18 is using multiplication: 3 × 3 × 2. And the only way for two 3s and a 2 to fit in this cage is for the 3s to be diagonally adjacent to each other and the 2 in the cell remaining. We can now deduce that the top number in the middle column must be 1, and that it is in a cage with a 3, since the only way to produce a 4 with two numbers in a row is 3 + 1 = 4. (You can also make 4 with two 2s, since 2 × 2 = 2 + 2 = 4, but this is not permitted here since both 2s would be in the same row.) The rest of the grid fills itself using the rule that each number

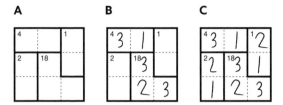

A   **B**   **C**

can only appear once in each column and row: the 1-cage uses subtraction, since 2 – 1 = 1, and the 2-cage division, since 2 ÷ 1 = 2 (or multiplication, since 2 × 1 = 2).

C. The completed grid.

➡ Miyamoto's first KenKens used only addition, and he included a '+' sign by the target number. He subsequently introduced cages using subtraction, multiplication and division, always including the relevant '–', '×' or '÷' so solvers knew which operation to use. Most KenKen that appear in Western publications include the signs by the target numbers. But Miyamoto also realized that it is possible to leave them out, which for me is when this puzzle gets really interesting. KenKens become more elegant, an extra layer is added for the solver, and they are more satisfying to complete. All the examples I have chosen are sign-free. Above the grid, however, is a reminder of the numbers to be used and the operations allowed.

When you solve a KenKen you can get a sense of what Miyamoto's classes must be like. The puzzles rely on arithmetic but in no way does solving them feel like a dull arithmetical chore. The dance between the logic and the arithmetic is magical, and there's the added charm of filling a grid so the numbers appear only once in each row and column – the pattern mathematicians call a Latin square. Sudoku was wise to the charms of the Latin square too!

I find KenKen surprisingly versatile, especially as the grids get bigger and new numbers come in. KenKen forces you to familiarize yourself with the properties of numbers, especially how they multiply and divide, since multiplication is usually the key to filling in the first cells of the grid. KenKen is an amazing puzzle: simple and deep. I've included quite challenging ones here. Keep on going until the end. Miyamoto offers some encouragement: 'When you solve [No.10] you can see a beautiful scene of numbers,' he says.

1 /  (1 - 4 , + , − , × , ÷)

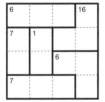

2 / (1 - 4 , + , − , × , ÷)

3 / (1 - 4 , + , − , × , ÷)

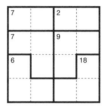

4 / (1 - 4 , + , − , × , ÷)

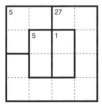

5 / (1 - 5 , + , − , × , ÷)

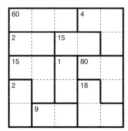

6 / 🥷🥷 (1-6, +, −, ×, ÷)

108		6		50	
	30	7		2	
			11		72
9		7			
1			6	12	5
	30				

7 / 🥷🥷 (1-7, +, −, ×, ÷)

18	42		9		3	
		2	9	14		11
	20			6		
24		2			11	
	24		21		30	6
	42	20				
			70			

8 / 🥷🥷🥷 (1-8, +, −, ×, ÷)

21		30	36		40	14	7
7	60						
		28		14			
2	48	42		7			15
	20		280				
84	6				10		15
	56	3		30			
4		24			24		

9 / 🥷🥷🥷 (1-9,+,−,×,÷)

36	14		8	24		24	24
			36		280	210	
28		1					
45	24	2		13	13		4
	15				9		
15	3		42	45			12
	4		7	112		17	
54		20					12
	2	63		15			

10 / 🥷🥷🥷 (1-10,+,−,×,÷)

17496			5488		1600	21	
	243		6				
25600	9	78732	12		3136		
						9	
196	112	2560	18		52488		
						81	

172

THE
YOUNG
SAMURAI

The Japanese logic puzzle scene is indebted to the US not only because its most famous creations, Sudoku and Kakuro, are refinements of American inventions, but also because of the geeky internationalism of the American puzzle king.

Will Shortz was the first – and is still the only – person to hold a university degree in enigmatology, the study of puzzles, which he graduated in after designing his own course at Indiana University in 1974. He is a household name in America, where entire shelves at bookstores creak with his crossword, Sudoku and other puzzle books, of which he has written over a hundred. (His own shelves creak with more than 25,000 books and magazines, the largest puzzle library in the world.) He is the crossword editor of the *New York Times*, and for the last three decades has posed weekly puzzles on NPR national radio.

Shortz's importance to Japan is that he is also the founder of the World Puzzle Championship (WPC), an annual event designed to enable contestants who do not speak the same language to solve puzzles on a level playing field. The first WPC took place in New York in 1992. As it has grown it has spawned an Olympics-style movement of global and national federations – the World Puzzle Federation now has thirty-three affiliated countries – whose competitions are essentially a showcase for new logic grid puzzles. Most of these, if not originally from Japan, are certainly inspired by Japan.

'We're living in the golden age of puzzle invention, with new ideas flying around the world all the time,' says Shortz.

Japan has taken part in the WPC since its inception, although it was not until 2010 that one of its countrymen, Taro Arimatsu, then aged 49, won the individual category for the first time.

Five years later, 22-year-old engineer Ken Endo became the second Japanese to win the WPC individual title.

Endo's social life revolves around competitive puzzling. I meet him and a group of his friends in a Tokyo bar where we drink beer and snack on *soramame*, broad beans barbecued in their pod. Still on the subject of legumes, the word *endo* means green pea in Japanese, which is why Ken decided on Edamame, or soyabean pod, for his puzzle *nom de guerre*. With us are Gomatamago, which means sesame egg (a Tokyo treat in which sesame seed and sweet bean paste is encased in a white chocolate shell); nyoroppyi, which means wriggler; Eden, which means Eden; and the only one who uses his real name, Takeya Saikachi.

A few years ago, Saikachi had the idea to start a fanzine for the Japanese competitive puzzle community. He wanted it to feature types of puzzle that had been devised for the WPC and other competitions like the Japanese Puzzle Championship, and thus become a platform for edgier, more experimental puzzles than those available in mainstream magazines. The first issue of *Toketa?* ('Solved?') came out in 2013. It has *six* difficulty levels: easy, normal, hard, very hard, super hard and impossible.

Toketa? has invented new puzzles, and also rescued many excellent puzzles from obscurity, dusting them off and giving them interesting new twists. 'It is meaningful for us to rediscover forgotten puzzles,' says Saikachi. In fact, the care with which *Toketa?* finds puzzles, traces their histories, suggests improvements and reveals solving methods has turned the magazine into something like the house journal of the international WPC community.

The ten puzzle creators who write all of *Toketa?*'s puzzles include my five companions. They say that they want to provide a service to members of the public who are sick of Sudoku. 'It's not that Sudoku is bad or boring, but because it just uses numbers the grids don't look very interesting,' says nyoroppyi. 'You don't get a surprise from Sudoku.'

Gomatamago adds: 'We try to create puzzles that have an element of surprise. Some puzzles you think, "Wow! There is a path like this!" And that's a good feeling.'

I promise that good feelings abound in the puzzles I have selected from *Toketa?* that follow in this chapter.

Wolves & Sheep
Slitherlink 狼と羊のスリザーリンク
DAVE TULLER, 2009

The challenge: Complete the Slitherlink grid, keeping all the sheep inside the loop and all the wolves outside it.

The rules: For Slitherlink rules see page 8.

How to solve it:

A. The starting grid.

B. Using basic Slitherlink knowledge we can mark little crosses around the 0s, where we know there are no lines. The loop has only one way to go around the 3, and we can extend it a few more cells where its path is determined. Since wolves are outside the loop and sheep inside it, whenever a wolf is adjacent to a sheep, the loop must pass between them.

C. Look at the 2-cell in the second column. We already know it has a line along its bottom side. The second line around this cell is either on the right side or the top side. If it were on the right side, however, the loop would have to stay on the right side of the sheep above the cell, meaning that the sheep would be outside the loop, which is forbidden. So the line must be along the top of the 2-cell.

Now look at the cell with the sheep in the bottom right corner. The loop already passes up the left side of this cell. Since all sheep must be inside the loop, the loop must also pass along the bottom and right side of this cell. If it didn't pass through these sides, there is no way for the sheep to be in the loop. The loop cannot separate two adjacent wolves, since this would mean one is inside the loop and one is outside it, so we can extend the loop up past the

A **B** **C**

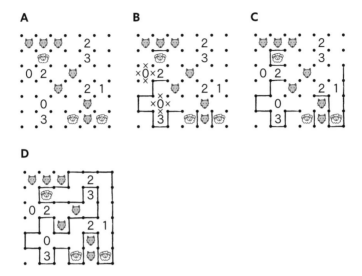

D

second wolf, to the left of the corner sheep. This extension means that we can continue the loop for three cells up the right side of the grid, since this is the only possible path.

With these fragments filled in, the rest of the loop emerges by filling in the only possible path that it can go. Remember that once you know which side of a line is inside the loop, and which side is outside it, you must extend it so all wolves are outside and all sheep inside.

D. The completed grid.

→ My first example from *Toketa?* is a charming twist on the *Nikoli* classic that opens this book. The idea of placing sheep in a Slitherlink puzzle was first suggested by the Japanese creator SAE in 2003. Wolves arrived six years later, in a single grid provided by an American puzzlist called Dave Tuller for the 2009 US Puzzle Championship, although in his grid the sheep and the wolves were denoted by an S and a W. *Toketa?* introduced the cute animal icons and have explored many fun patterns. Edamame wrote problem 6, for example, which is inspired by the Japanese solitaire card game Shephy, in which one starts with a single sheep in a field and must grow the flock to a thousand-strong. The Shephy pack has 22 'action' cards, and 'sheep' cards for 1, 3, 10, 30, 100, 300 and 1,000 sheep, which is why Edamame placed 22 wolves in the grid, and placed the numbers 1, 3, 10, 30, 100, 300 and 1,000 each next to a sheep. No woolly thinking here!

1/ EDEN

2/ TAKEYA SAIKACHI

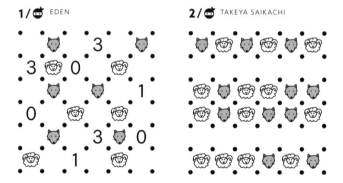

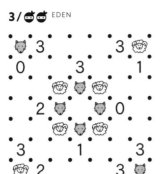
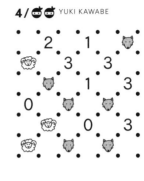

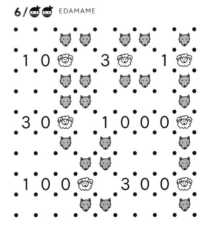

7/ 🥷🥷 GOMATAMAGO

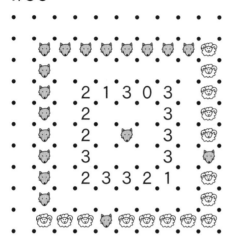

8/ 🥷🥷🥷 TAKEYA SAIKACHI

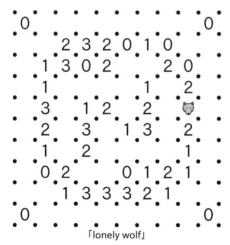

「lonely wolf」

9/  SHINICHI AOKI

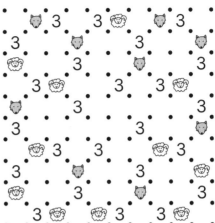

10/ EDEN

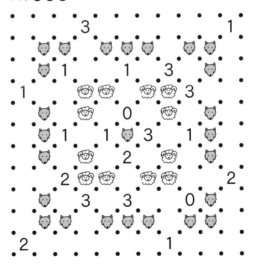

Skyscrapers ビルディング

MASANORI NATSUHARA, 1992

The challenge: Fill the grid with numbers, so that every number appears only once in every row and column. The numbers used range from 1 up to the length of each row or column.

The rules: Imagine the grid is the aerial view of a city block of skyscrapers of varying heights, one within each cell in the grid. Each skyscraper is to be represented by a number indicating its height. A number *outside* the grid describes how many skyscrapers can be seen along that row or up/down that column from the perspective of that number on the ground. You can only see a skyscraper if smaller skyscrapers are in front of it; you cannot see one if a taller skyscraper is in front of it, blocking the view.

How to solve it:

A. The starting grid.
B. The obvious places to start are either where there is a 4, meaning we can see all four skyscrapers, or where there is a 1, meaning we can see only one. If we can see every skyscraper they must be arranged in ascending order, so the view from the 4 on the second row must go 1-2-3-4. Likewise, the only way to see a single skyscraper is if the highest comes first, so we can put a 4 above the 1 on the bottom row, since the view from that 1 goes up the second column.
C. With two 4s already in the grid, there are only two positions left for the 4 on the top row: in the first or the third column. We can eliminate the latter since a 4 here would mean it is impossible to see three skyscrapers looking along the top row from the 3. So the 4 is in the first column and the final 4 in the grid must be row three, column three.

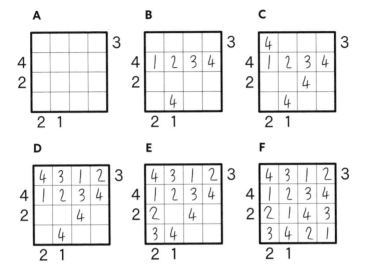

D. In order to see three skyscrapers from 3, one of them must be hidden. The order for the row must be either 4-2-3-1, 4-1-3-2 or 4-3-1-2. We can eliminate the first one since this doubles up 2s in the second column, and we can eliminate the second since this doubles up 3s on the third column. So the order is 4-3-1-2.

E. In order to see only two skyscrapers up the first column, a 3 must be in the bottom cell. The rest of the grid now fills itself based on the rule that every number appears once on each row and column.

F. The completed grid.

1 / 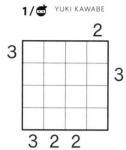 YUKI KAWABE

2 / YUKI KAWABE

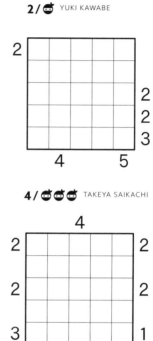

3 / EDEN

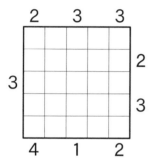

4 / TAKEYA SAIKACHI

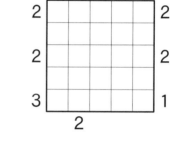

5 / SHINICHI AOKI

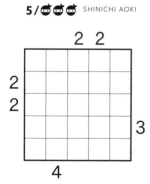

Puzzler magazine published the first Skyscrapers puzzle in 1992 in its page for readers' submissions, and it soon became a classic. It spread around the world thanks to the WPC. It is an elegantly simple idea, relying – like Sudoku and KenKen – on the Latin square, that is, the requirement that numbers appear only once in any row and column. This requirement gives these puzzles an inner harmony and intuitively understandable rules. What I find particularly enjoyable about Skyscrapers is the way it forces me to think in three dimensions, as if the puzzle is popping up off the page.

The following puzzle is a variation on Skyscrapers, which retains the flavor of the original while relying on different strategies. It was a modification devised by the Dutchman Tim Peeters and included in the 2003 WPC.

Sum Skyscrapers サム・ビルディング

TIM PEETERS, 2003

The challenge: Fill the grid with numbers, so that every number appears only once in every row and column. The numbers used are 1 up to the length of each row or column.

The rules: The same as for Skyscrapers, except that a number outside the grid now describes the *sum* of the heights of the skyscrapers that can be seen along that row or column from the perspective of that number. So, if a skyscraper is hidden behind a taller one, we do not count the height of the smaller skyscraper in the sum.

How to solve it:

A. The starting grid.

B. First let's calculate the maximum sum of heights, which we would get if all skyscrapers were visible. The maximum sum is $1 + 2 + 3 + 4 = 10$. The second row has a 10, so we can deduce that the view from there is 1-2-3-4.

C. There are only two ways to sum 7 using the numbers 1, 2, 3 and 4 at most once each: either $1 + 2 + 4$, or $3 + 4$. In other words, the view from a 7 will either be skyscrapers of height 1, 2 and 4, or skyscrapers of height 3 and 4. The combination 1-2-4 is not possible for the 7 in the first column, since the skyscraper in the first row will block the view of the 1 in the second row. So the view from the 7 in the first column is 3-4, which means that the first cell is a 3. The first cell in the second column cannot be a 3, since the top row already has a 3, so the view from the 7 in the second column must be 1-2-4, and the only way to make this the case is for the column to be 1-2-4-3. We can now complete the final two cells in the first column: 3-1-2-4.

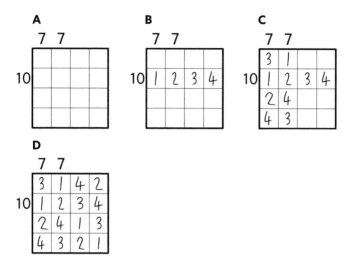

The rest of the grid can now be filled in Sudoku-style, following the rule that every number must appear once in every row and column.

D. The completed grid.

1/ 🥷 EDAMAME

5 6 7 8 9

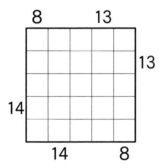

2/ 🥷 SERKAN YÜREKLI

8   13

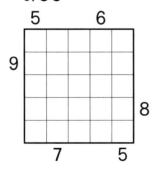

3/ 🥷🥷 SERKAN YÜREKLI

5   6

4 /  SHINICHI AOKI

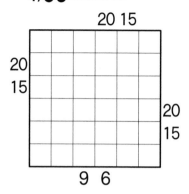

5 / SERKAN YÜREKLI

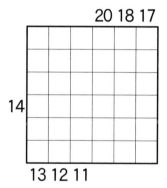

Edamame 枝豆

ATSUMI HIROSE, 2014

The challenge: Place edamame bean pods on the grid.

The rules: An edamame pod is a rectangle at least three cells long that contains exactly three beans: one at each end and one in another cell. Pods cannot overlap or cover numbered cells. The number in a cell denotes the number of beans in the cells horizontally or vertically adjacent to it. Not all cells need to be covered by pods or numbers: all these remaining cells must form a single continuous region, meaning that these white cells are connected together horizontally and/or vertically.

How to solve it:

A. The starting grid.
B. There are only two free positions for beans next to the 2 on the top row, and only three free positions next to the 3 on the second row. So we can place beans on these free cells.
C. The only possible edamame pod for the bean above the 3 is a three-cell horizontal pod, so we can draw it in. The other three free beans must be in vertical pods.
D. The free bean in the middle column must be in a pod that extends downwards, but this pod cannot extend to the bottom edge of the grid, since if it did it would mean that the white cells in the grid are split into two regions, which is forbidden. So this pod must be three cells long, with a bean in each cell. The 2-cell in the second row must be adjacent to two beans. We know it has a bean to its right. We can now deduce that it cannot have a bean underneath it, since this bean would have to be in a pod and there is no way to place a pod (which contains three beans) such that this bean is included. So the

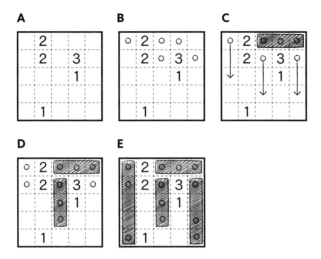

A **B** **C**

D **E**

lower 2-cell's second bean must be to its left. In the final column, there can be no bean to the right of the 1-cell, since this cell's bean is already taken, so the two remaining beans of the pod must be in the bottom two cells. From this it follows that the 1 on the bottom line must have a bean to its left.

E. The completed grid.

➡ If you thought that you couldn't get more Japanese than a logic puzzle about a grid of skyscrapers, think again! Edamame could only be more Japanese if you played it with green soyabean pods in a bento box. The puzzle was invented by Atsumi Hirose, who also uses the pen-name Acetonitrile, and who co-invented the *Nikoli* classic Masyu. He is one of the founder members of *Toketa?*, and he says the idea for this puzzle was triggered by Ken Endo's pseudonym, Edamame. In problems 4 and 5 a bean is already placed in the starting grids.

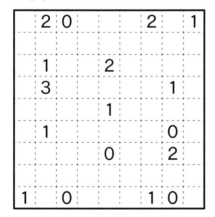

1						2	
		2					0
1					0		
		2					
2			0				1
				2			
	1						1
1				1			
	1						0

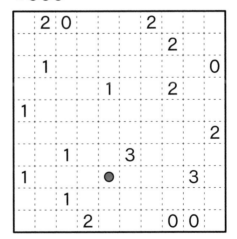

5 / 🥷🥷🥷🥷 GOMATAMAGO

1					1		2	
	2		2		2			
		3				●		1
	1		3					
					3		2	
2						1		
			1		1		2	
	1		1					1

6 / 🥷🥷🥷🥷 EDAMAME

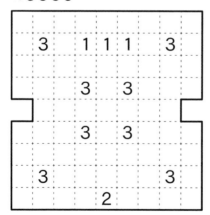

Slash Pack スラッシュパック

YOSUKE IMAI, 2007

The challenge: Divide the grid into regions that include each of the given numbers only once, drawing dividing lines diagonally across unnumbered cells.

The rules: Each cell can contain only one diagonal line. Some cells may be left completely empty.

How to solve it:

A. The starting grid.

B. A region cannot contain the same number more than once, so there must be a border between the two diagonally adjacent 3s to make sure they are in different regions.

C. There is no way of separating the 1, 2 and 3 on the top row into different regions, so they must be in the same region, and there is only one way to complete that region using diagonals. There is no way of separating the 3 and 1 on the second row, nor is there a way of separating the 1 and 2 on the third row. Since they both include a 1 these doubles must be in separate regions. So we can draw a separating diagonal in the empty cell between them.

D. Now look at 1 and 2 on the third row – there are two choices for which 3 will be in their region. It must be the 3 in the bottom left, since it is impossible to include the other 3 in the region without also including a second 2. The 3 and the 1 on the second row must be in the same region as the 2 in the final column, since there is no way to include the other 2 without also including another 3. Now that we know which numbers are grouped together, there is only one way to draw in the boundary.

E. The completed grid.

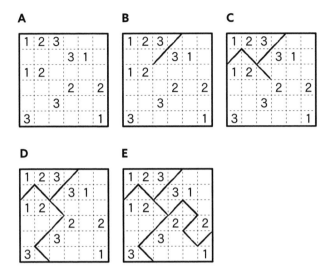

➥ When I asked Tetsuya Nishio from Chapter 2 which puzzles in *Toketa?* he liked best, he said Slash Pack and Curve Data, which are the two final puzzles in this book. I find Slash Pack an incredible puzzle because it is so familiar and yet so different. The rules are similar to other standard puzzles in which you must divide the grid into regions. Yet by using only diagonals you have to completely relearn how to navigate across the cells. Drawing in the jagged borders really does feel like you are slashing through the page with a knife. Remember, some squares can be left empty. Slash Pack was invented by Yosuke Imai and first appeared in the qualification round for the 2007 Japanese Puzzle Championship.

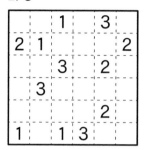

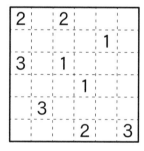

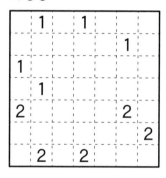

	2		3		2		
1						3	
	1		3			1	
			2		1		
2	3						3
		3			1		
1			2				
		1		3	2		2

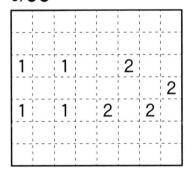

7/ GOMATAMAGO

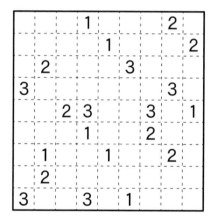

8/ SHINICHI AOKI

204

9 / 🐡🐡🐡 SERKAN YÜREKLI

				3	4		
		3	2		4		
5							
		2	1		3		
				1			
		4			5		
					2		
	5						
			1				

10 / 🐡🐡🐡🐡 GOMATAMAGO

1	1	3	4	4
2	2	4	1	1
2	3		3	2
3	2	2	3	1
1	4	3	4	4

Curve Data カーブデータ

TATSUYA YAMAMOTO, 2002

The challenge: Stretch the shapes so that they cover every cell in the grid.

The rules: The shapes are made up of horizontal and vertical lines. Horizontal lines can be stretched only horizontally, and vertical lines stretched only vertically. Each line segment of the stretched shape must be at least one cell long, but the amount stretched can vary. All the angles in each shape must be preserved after stretching. The stretched shape must pass through the cell with the original shape. Only one line passes through each cell.

How to solve it:

A. The starting grid.

B. We start building the stretched shapes, segment by segment. The middle shape, a typewriter-style 1, has a horizontal line as a base. This horizontal line cannot be in the cell of the shape, since the line must be at least a cell long and it cannot pass through the cells containing shapes on either side. Nor can it be above this cell, since if it was there would be no way for the stretched shape to go through the original cell. So the line must go below the original cell, and the vertical line of the 1-shape must go through that cell.

C. The lines we have drawn affect how we can stretch the other shapes. The 0 and the 2 shapes must expand in the way illustrated if they are to include the original cells.

D. The 2-shape has a tail that turns upwards. This tail must stretch upwards by at least one cell, and if it does, the vertical part of the 2-shape must also stretch upwards by a cell if it is to be completed without overlapping. The 1-shape must also stretch up a cell, since it will need to extend left.

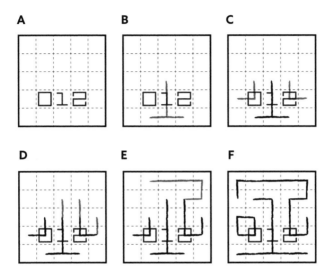

A B C

D E F

E. The 1-shape needs to stretch at least one cell to the left to replicate the top of the shape. There is only one way now for the 2-shape to continue before its final, downward segment.

F. The completed grid.

➡ Founder *Toketa?* member Tatsuya Yamamoto wanted to devise a puzzle that uses shape as the key to solving it. So he came up with Curve Data. He could have called it, say, 'Slime Stretcher', which is definitely catchier, and possibly more representative of the solving experience. The idea behind the puzzle, however, is contained in the original name. In math, pretty much any kind of line, even with straight bits, is called a curve, so the figures we are stretching are curves. These curves encode information, or 'data', such as the relative positions of the 90-degree turns. The puzzle is therefore asking us to stretch curves in such a way that maintains the data. Curve Data is a lovely introduction to the field of topology, the math of geometrical properties that do not change under stretching.

To fill in the grids, you will need to exercise your spatial intuition in a way you have not used previously in this book. The rules seem a bit cumbersome when explained with words, even though the idea is simple to understand visually. Your brain - as well as the figures in the grid - will be stretched in different directions, but I promise it is more than worth the contortions.

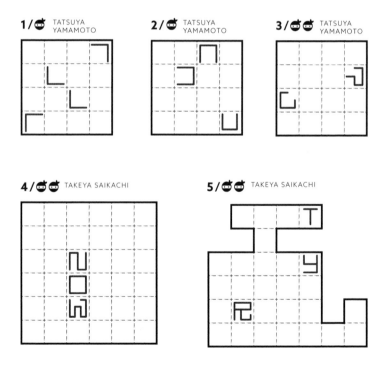

1 / TATSUYA YAMAMOTO

2 / TATSUYA YAMAMOTO

3 / TATSUYA YAMAMOTO

4 / TAKEYA SAIKACHI

5 / TAKEYA SAIKACHI

6 / 🥷🥷 TATSUYA YAMAMOTO

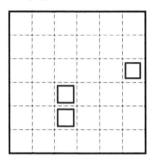

7 / 🥷🥷 TATSUYA YAMAMOTO

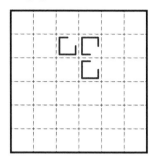

8 / 🥷🥷🥷 GOMATAMAGO

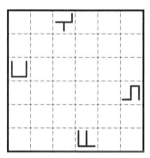

9 / 🥷🥷🥷 TATSUYA YAMAMOTO

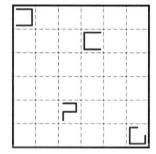

10 / 🥷🥷🥷 TATSUYA YAMAMOTO

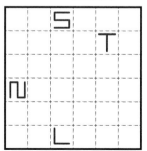

CONCLUSION

You came, you concentrated, you scribbled. You concentrated, you erased, and you scribbled again.

In these pages we have drawn loops, shaded triangles, arranged panels, spun shapes, stretched figures and revealed pictures. We have created islands, filled rooms, encircled sheep and putted balls into holes. Our eyes have scanned cells horizontally, vertically and diagonally. We have envisaged the grid in two *and* three dimensions.

Yes, it's been a workout for the brain (and thumb and forefinger), but it has also been a thrilling journey to discover the spectacular creativity of the Japanese puzzle scene. Jimmy Goto of *Nikoli* compared the grid logic puzzle to a *hakoniwa* miniature garden. To extend the metaphor, we have seen an extravagant and seemingly inexhaustible variety of small but perfectly formed horticultural wonders.

Researching this book I was endlessly delighted and surprised by the different flavors of experience each puzzle provides, despite the fact they are all based on square grids of roughly the same size, and all have simple, often quite similar rules. To come up with an interesting and challenging puzzle based on nothing more than, for example, drawing a line through a cell is a spectacular achievement.

Quite why Japan became the world superpower of grid logic puzzles is in itself a puzzle not fully solved, not even by the puzzle masters I interviewed during my research. Perhaps it is because these beautiful, handcrafted puzzles resonate in a culture famous for beautiful, handcrafted objects. Perhaps solving puzzles fits in with national traits of perseverance and logical thinking. Perhaps it was sparked by the rivalry between two innovative puzzle magazines in the 1980s. Probably, it's a little bit of all these reasons.

Yet having spent hours and hours held in the grip of these puzzles I realize we learn from them as much about ourselves as we do anything about the Far East. We learn how we cope when faced with something we don't know. We learn how to search an opening grid for the first clues and how to build up an armory of strategies. We also learn to be patient and determined, and that if we trust our logical reasoning and take time we will eventually be able to reach the solution.

Most of all, however, we learn how enjoyable it is to be set a challenge and to overcome it. By the end of this book, your brain will have been twisted, squeezed and pummelled. But it will, I hope, also be permeated with pleasure and satisfaction.

ARIGATO

A massive thank you to everyone who helped me in Japan. I would not have been able to plan my trip without the guidance of the puzzle inventor and writer Hirokazu 'Iwahiro' Iwasawa, who was very generous with his knowledge and connections. Thanks to all the puzzle masters who gave me their time: Tetsuya Nishio, Naoki Inaba, Tetsuya Miyamoto, Ken Endo (Edamame), nyoroppyi, Gomatamago, Eden and Takeya Saikachi. The staff at *Nikoli*, especially Jimmy Goto and Yoshinao Anpuku, were incredibly helpful and accommodating, and Maki Kaji was lively and big-hearted as always.

I am grateful for the help I received from Wakaba Hoshino Miyamoto, Taro Arimatsu, Naoaki Takashima, Meiko Kimura of Torito, Yoshiyuki Kotani, Lumi Hosokawa at *Gakken* and Naoto Okamura. Thanks also to Pavel Curtis, James Dalgety, Robert Fuhrer of www.kenken.com, Phil McNeill, Will Shortz, David Singmaster, Jerry Slocum, Laura Taalman and Serkan Yürekli.

Laura Hassan was my ninja editor at Faber & Faber. A bow to her brilliant team: designer Anna Green; copy-editor Ben Sumner; proofreader Hamish Ironside; illustrator Darren Hughes; and Lindsay Davies who fearlessly made sure everything came together. At Faber: Lauren Nicoll in publicity, John Grindrod in marketing, Dave Watkins in pre-press and Jack Murphy in production.

Thanks to my agent Rebecca Carter at Janklow & Nesbit and her colleagues Kirsty Gordon, Rebecca Folland, Kate I'Anson and Rachel Balcombe.

Sumo-sized hugs to Natalie for her love and support, and for letting me spend so many evenings curled up on the sofa doing puzzles.

ANSWERS

The Puzzle Cavalry

SLITHERLINK

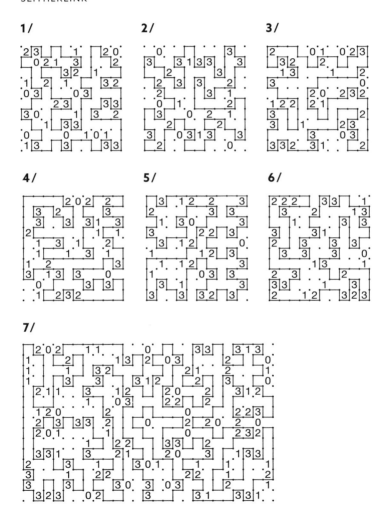

1/   2/   3/

4/   5/   6/

7/

8 /

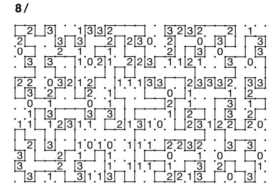

9 /

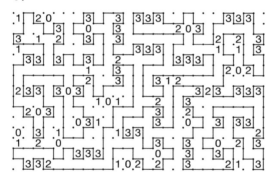

10/

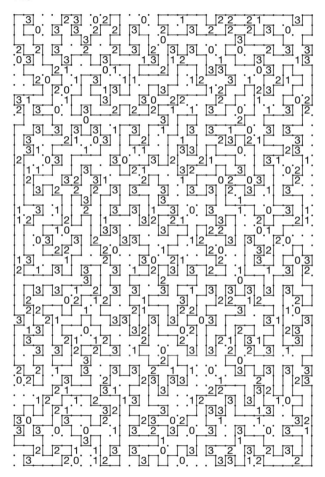

HASHIWOKAKERO

1/

2/

3/

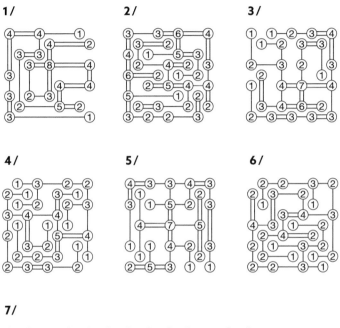

4/

5/

6/

7/

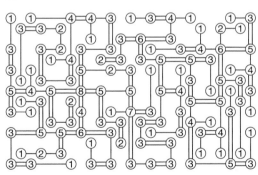

8/

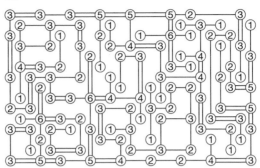

9/

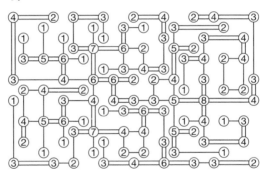

10/

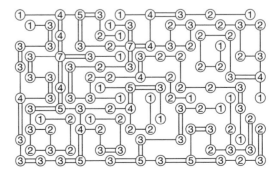

NURIKABE

1 / **2 /** **3 /**

4 / **5 /** **6 /**

7 / **8 /**

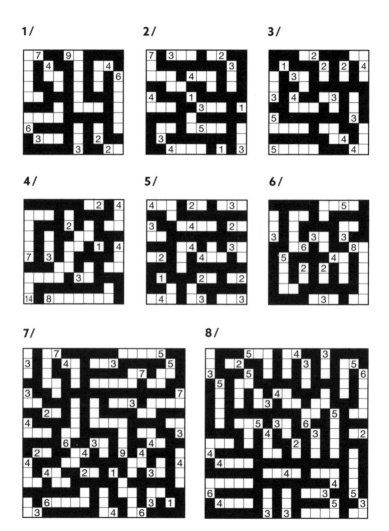

9/

10/

HEYAWAKE

1/ **2/** **3/**

4/ **5/** **6/**

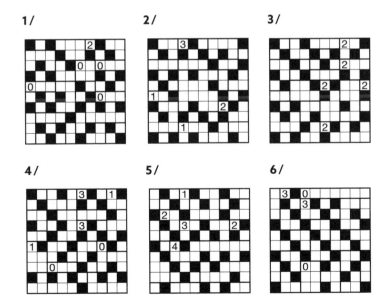

7/

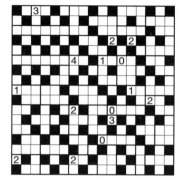

8/

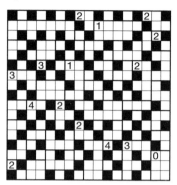

9/

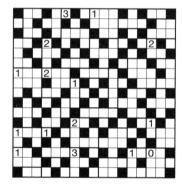

10/

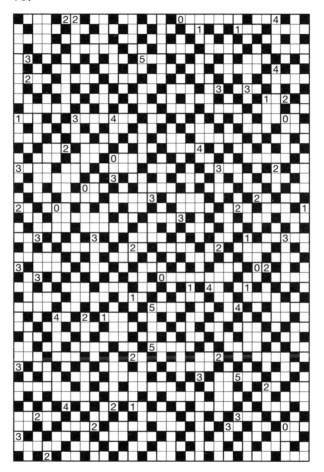

FILLOMINO

1/

```
8 8 1 8 8 8 1 6 6 6
2 8 8 8 1 2 2 6 5 6
2 4 2 1 7 7 7 7 5 6
4 4 2 7 7 2 2 5 5 1
4 3 3 7 4 6 6 5 1 4
2 2 3 4 4 1 6 4 4 4
1 8 1 3 4 3 6 6 2 3
8 8 3 3 6 3 1 6 2 3
8 2 2 1 6 3 5 5 5 3
8 8 8 8 6 6 6 6 5 5
```

2/

```
5 6 6 6 2 6 6 6 7 7
5 5 5 6 2 6 1 6 7 2
2 2 5 6 6 1 7 6 7 2
5 5 3 2 2 6 7 1 7 7
5 3 3 6 1 6 7 7 1 7
5 5 6 6 2 6 6 7 7 1
4 3 3 6 2 5 6 5 7 5
4 3 4 6 5 5 6 5 5 5
4 2 4 6 5 2 5 2 2 1
4 2 4 5 2 5 5 5 5 5
```

3/

```
1 3 3 4 4 4 4 3 3 3
2 2 3 2 2 1 2 2 4 4
3 3 6 3 3 4 4 1 4 1
6 3 6 6 3 4 2 5 4 5
6 4 4 6 1 4 2 5 5 5
6 6 4 6 4 5 5 1 3 3
4 6 4 6 4 5 6 6 1 3
4 6 3 4 4 5 5 6 3 1
4 4 3 3 6 3 3 6 3 3
6 6 6 6 6 3 6 6 2 2
```

4/

```
4 4 4 4 2 5 3 3 5 5
3 2 2 1 2 5 3 5 5 5
3 1 3 3 3 5 1 3 3 3
3 2 5 5 1 5 5 1 6 2
5 2 1 5 5 7 7 7 6 2
5 5 5 4 5 7 4 6 6 6
5 4 4 4 7 7 4 6 2 4
3 2 2 1 7 3 4 4 2 4
3 3 4 2 2 3 1 5 4 4
2 2 4 4 4 3 5 5 5 5
```

5/

```
4 4 4 4 1 4 4 1 4 4
3 3 3 1 4 4 1 4 2 4
2 4 4 3 3 2 2 4 2 4
2 4 4 3 4 4 1 1 4 3
3 3 1 4 1 4 4 5 1 3
3 4 4 4 2 5 5 5 5 3
1 2 2 3 2 4 4 4 2 1
4 3 1 3 3 2 2 4 2 3
4 3 3 4 4 3 3 1 3 3
4 4 1 4 4 3 4 4 4 4
```

6/

```
5 5 4 3 3 3 4 4 4 3
5 4 4 2 2 1 6 4 3 3
5 5 4 3 3 3 6 6 4 4
3 3 5 6 6 6 1 6 6 4
3 1 5 5 5 6 6 5 6 4
6 6 5 6 3 6 1 5 1 6
6 2 6 3 3 5 5 6 6 6
6 2 6 6 4 4 4 5 1 6
6 6 1 6 4 1 3 4 6 6
4 4 4 4 1 3 3 4 4 4
```

7/

```
1 3 3 3 7 4 4 4 2 4 4 4 7 1 6 6 1
4 4 4 4 7 2 2 4 2 4 7 7 7 2 2 6 3
3 3 1 3 7 7 3 3 7 7 7 2 2 1 6 6 3
3 4 4 3 3 7 7 3 1 4 2 4 5 2 2 6 3
5 5 4 4 1 7 1 7 7 4 2 4 5 5 5 2 1
7 5 7 7 7 1 2 7 2 4 7 4 5 5 5 2 1
7 5 5 1 7 7 2 7 2 4 7 4 2 2 3 2 3
7 1 2 2 7 1 7 3 7 7 7 7 3 3 4 3 3
7 5 5 5 2 3 7 7 3 3 2 2 7 4 4 4 3
7 5 3 3 2 3 3 1 7 7 7 3 1 3 3 1 4
7 5 3 1 6 6 1 3 7 2 7 3 7 3 2 4 4
7 6 6 6 1 6 3 3 7 2 7 3 7 7 2 4 1
3 3 3 6 4 6 6 2 3 3 3 7 1 7 7 7 7
2 5 6 6 4 4 6 2 5 2 7 7 7 2 1 5 3
2 5 5 5 4 5 5 5 2 5 5 7 2 5 5 5 3
5 1 4 4 2 2 5 2 5 5 1 7 5 5 1 3
5 5 5 5 4 3 3 3 2 5 2 2 7 3 3 3 1
```

8/

```
5 5 5 1 2 3 4 1 2 3 4 5 3 3 6 6
7 3 5 4 2 3 4 4 2 3 4 5 3 2 2 6
7 3 4 4 3 5 3 4 1 4 3 4 5 5 3 6 6
7 3 7 3 3 5 5 3 4 4 1 4 5 1 3 3 6
7 7 7 6 5 5 2 3 4 3 3 1 3 3 2 2 3
6 6 6 6 6 4 2 3 1 3 4 3 1 3 4 3 3
5 5 5 5 5 4 7 6 4 4 4 3 3 1 4 4 4
4 4 4 4 1 4 7 6 6 6 6 4 4 4 6 6 6
3 3 3 1 7 4 7 6 5 5 5 4 6 6 6 4 4
4 4 4 4 7 7 7 5 2 2 5 1 3 3 4 4 6
5 5 5 5 5 2 2 5 6 4 5 4 3 6 6 6 6
6 6 6 6 6 5 5 5 6 4 1 4 4 6 4 4 4
7 7 7 6 2 2 6 6 6 4 5 1 4 1 4 6 6
7 2 2 4 4 4 1 6 4 5 4 1 3 3 3 6
7 7 15 5 5 5 5 4 4 3 5 4 3 4 1 1 6 6
7 2 2 6 6 3 2 4 2 3 5 4 3 4 4 4 6
6 6 6 6 3 3 2 4 2 3 5 4 3 1 3 3 3
```

9/

```
1 2 3 3 3 7 7 7 7 7 7 1 5 4 4 4
4 2 4 4 4 2 2 3 3 2 2 7 5 5 3 4
4 4 2 4 5 5 5 7 7 7 7 7 5 2 3 1
4 1 2 5 5 2 2 3 3 3 2 2 4 5 2 3
2 2 1 2 2 7 7 7 7 7 7 4 7 7 1 2
3 5 2 5 5 2 2 3 3 3 2 2 4 4 7 3
3 5 2 1 5 5 5 7 7 1 7 7 7 7 4 3
3 5 5 1 2 2 1 7 1 2 2 3 3 3 4 1
4 4 4 4 5 5 1 7 7 7 5 5 5 5 4 4
5 2 5 5 5 2 2 3 3 3 2 2 7 7 2 1
5 2 6 6 6 6 6 7 7 1 1 7 7 3 3 2
5 5 6 4 4 2 2 1 7 1 2 2 7 7 3 5
5 3 3 3 4 4 1 7 7 1 3 3 3 2 2 5
2 2 4 2 1 2 2 3 3 3 2 2 5 5 3 4
1 4 4 2 7 7 1 7 7 7 5 5 5 3 3 4
2 1 2 2 7 7 1 7 7 7 6 6 6 6 3 3
```

10/

```
2 1 2 3 3 3 7 3 3 3 1 3 3 5 5 5
2 3 2 6 6 6 7 7 7 3 2 3 2 2 5 1
3 3 1 6 1 6 6 3 7 3 3 2 6 5 5 1 5
4 4 3 3 3 2 3 3 7 6 6 6 6 5 1 5 5
4 4 1 2 1 2 1 2 3 6 8 2 3 5 5 1 5
5 3 3 2 3 3 3 2 3 8 8 2 3 3 1 4 5
5 3 5 5 1 1 6 6 6 3 8 1 8 1 5 5 4 4
5 5 6 5 5 6 3 3 5 8 8 8 5 5 7 7 4
1 5 6 5 6 6 3 4 5 5 1 1 3 3 5 8 7 7
5 6 6 6 3 3 4 4 5 8 8 8 3 8 8 8 7
5 6 1 3 1 3 1 4 5 4 4 8 1 2 1 8 7
5 5 5 3 2 2 5 5 4 4 8 8 8 2 8 8 7
2 2 1 3 1 3 1 5 5 8 1 8 1 8 1 8 3
5 5 5 2 2 3 2 5 2 8 8 2 8 8 8 2 3
5 4 5 3 1 3 1 2 8 1 2 8 1 2 1 8 3
4 4 3 3 5 5 5 4 4 8 8 4 4 8 8 3 1
4 2 2 1 5 1 5 1 1 4 4 8 8 4 4 8 3 3
```

YAJILIN

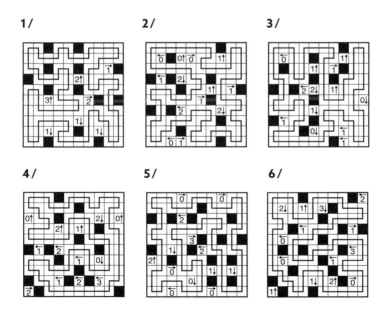

1/ 2/ 3/

4/ 5/ 6/

7/

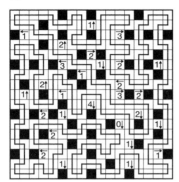

8/

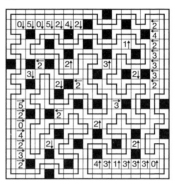

9/

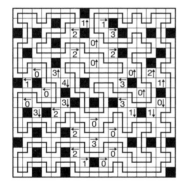

10/

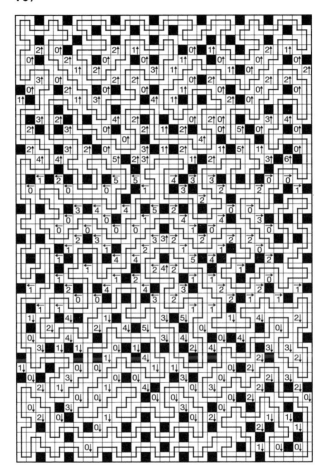

MASYU

1/　　　　　　**2/**　　　　　　**3/**

4/　　　　　　**5/**　　　　　　**6/**

7/　　　　　　**8/**

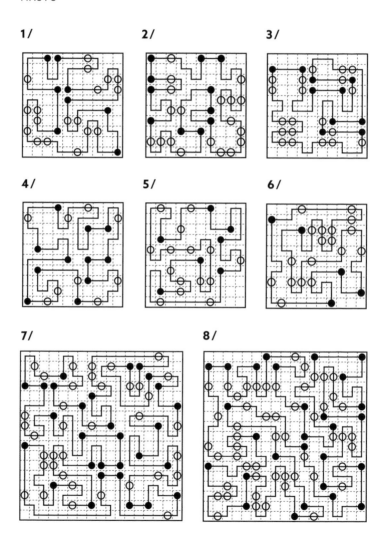

9/

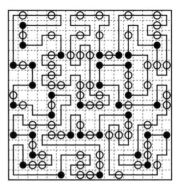

10/

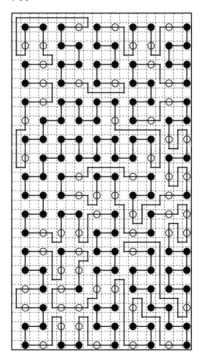

TENTAI SHOW

1/

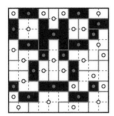

2/

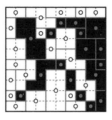

3/

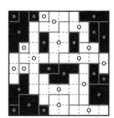

4/

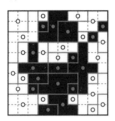

5/

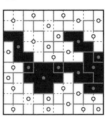

6/

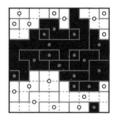

7/

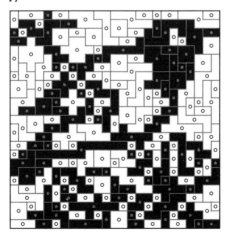

8 /

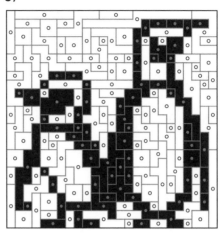

9 /

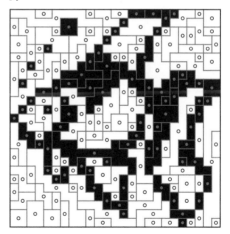

10/

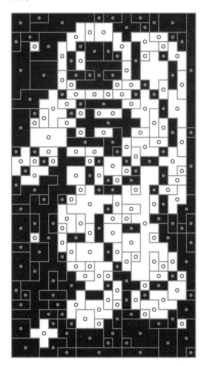

SHAKASHAKA

1/   **2/**   **3/**

4/   **5/**   **6/**

7/

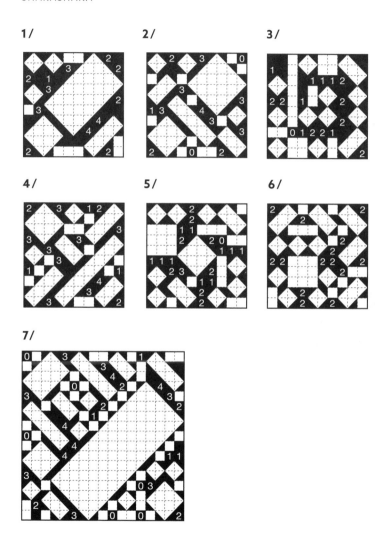

8 /

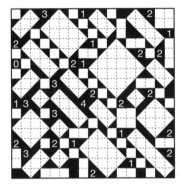

9 /

10/

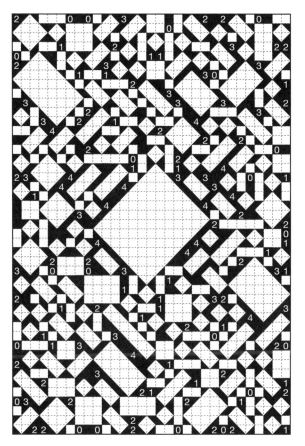

HERUGOLF

1/   **2/**   **3/**

4/   **5/**   **6/**

7/   **8/**

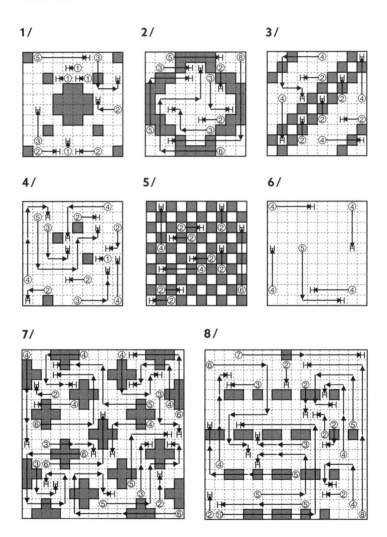

9/

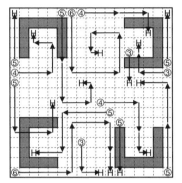

10/

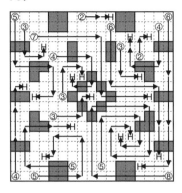

The Puzzle Poet

O'EKAKI

1 / MINUS MAN

2 / LOOK THIS WAY!

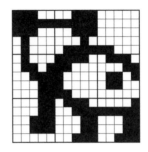

3 / ONE OF FOUR KINGS

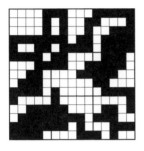

4 / A JAPANESE BEAUTY

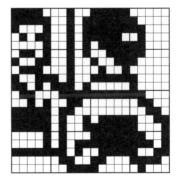

5 / LAZYBONES!

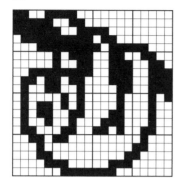

The Warrior Monk

L-PANEL

1/

2/

3/

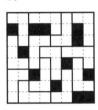

4/

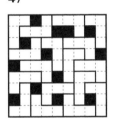

5/

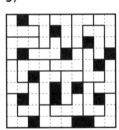

6/

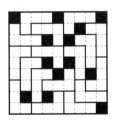

7/

8 /

MARUPEKE

1 /

2 /

3 /

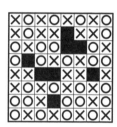

4 /

5 /

BLOCK NUMBER

1/

1	3	1	5	3
2	4	2	4	1
1	3	1	3	2
2	4	5	4	1
5	1	2	3	2

2/

3	1	2	4	2	1
2	5	3	1	5	3
4	1	4	2	4	2
3	2	3	1	3	1
4	1	5	4	2	4
2	3	2	1	3	1

3/

1	3	2	3	1	4	2
5	4	1	5	2	3	1
3	2	3	4	1	4	2
1	5	1	2	3	5	3
2	3	4	5	1	2	1
4	1	2	3	4	3	4
2	5	4	1	2	1	2

4/

1	5	2	1	4	3	4	1
2	3	4	3	2	1	2	3
4	1	2	1	4	3	4	1
2	3	4	3	2	1	2	3
4	1	2	1	5	3	5	4
2	3	5	3	4	1	2	1
1	4	1	2	5	3	4	5
3	2	3	4	1	2	1	2

STRAIGHT CROSS

1/ **2/** **3/**

4/ **5/**

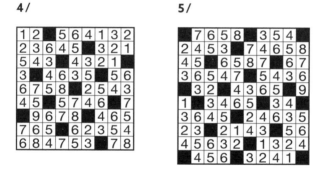

WALLS

1/

2/

3/

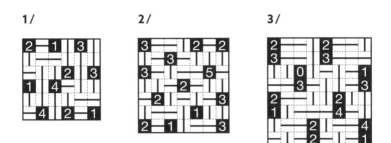

4/

5/

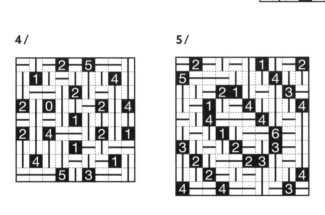

6 /

7 /

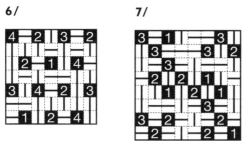

8 /

9 /

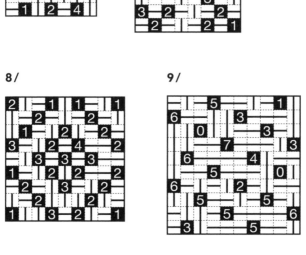

SEARCHLIGHTS

1/

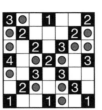

2/

3/

4/

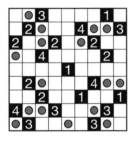

5/

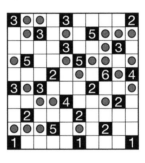

REN-KATSU

1/

```
4 4 4 1 4 2
1 2 3 5 3 5
3 2 1 3 1 2
1 5 6 2 6 5
4 2 3 1 4 1
6 1 3 2 3 2
```

2/

```
2 5 2 4 5 1 2
3 5 3 4 1 2 1
2 1 4 2 2 6 3
1 6 3 4 3 5 1
5 4 5 1 2 3 2
1 2 3 6 1 3 1
4 1 5 4 1 4 2
```

3/

```
2 2 5 1 5 1 3 1
1 3 6 3 6 2 4 6
3 2 4 1 4 1 2 1
4 3 5 6 1 5 1 5
1 2 1 3 4 1 4 1
6 5 4 2 3 2 3 6
1 6 5 4 5 1 5 1
4 2 3 1 6 1 6 1
```

4/

```
1 2 3 4 5 6 7 8 9
2 4 2 3 4 5 6 7 6
4 5 1 2 1 2 8 1 7
5 3 1 1 2 1 4 6 8
6 5 5 6 6 4 2 9 2
3 3 5 6 9 3 1 3 4
3 2 1 7 8 1 3 4 5
2 1 2 3 3 2 5 2 1
1 4 4 3 3 1 2 5 3
```

5/

```
8 2 4 2 6 3 2 5 1 3
1 5 6 1 2 1 7 4 2 1
7 3 1 3 5 2 6 1 3 4
4 5 3 6 1 4 3 2 7 5
1 3 4 2 9 9 4 5 8 3
7 1 2 3 9 9 2 4 6 4
4 5 3 4 6 5 4 6 1 3
5 2 1 5 4 2 3 1 3 2
6 1 2 7 2 3 1 6 7 1
8 5 7 4 3 1 2 8 5 4
```

STONES

1/

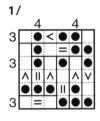

2/

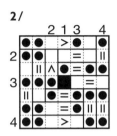

3/

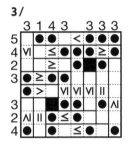

4/

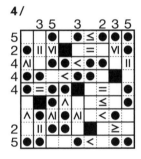

5/

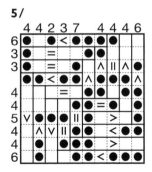

The Super Sensei

KENKEN

1/

2	1	3	4
3	2	4	1
4	3	1	2
1	4	2	3

2/

3	4	2	1
2	3	1	4
1	2	4	3
4	1	3	2

3/

2	4	3	1
1	3	2	4
4	2	1	3
3	1	4	2

4/

3	1	4	2
1	3	2	4
4	2	1	3
2	4	3	1

5/

5	3	4	1	2
4	2	3	5	1
3	1	2	4	5
2	5	1	3	4
1	4	5	2	3

6/

3	6	1	4	5	2
6	3	4	1	2	5
5	2	3	6	1	4
4	1	2	5	6	3
1	4	5	2	3	6
2	5	6	3	4	1

7/

5	2	7	3	6	1	4
6	3	1	4	7	2	5
7	4	2	5	1	3	6
1	5	3	6	2	4	7
2	6	4	7	3	5	1
3	7	5	1	4	6	2
4	1	6	2	5	7	3

8/

3	7	5	6	1	8	2	4
8	4	2	3	6	5	7	1
1	5	3	4	7	6	8	2
4	8	6	7	2	1	3	5
2	6	4	5	8	7	1	3
7	3	1	2	5	4	6	8
6	2	8	1	4	3	5	7
5	1	7	8	3	2	4	6

9/

2	5	9	1	8	3	6	4	7
3	6	1	2	9	4	7	5	8
4	7	2	3	1	5	8	6	9
5	8	3	4	2	6	9	7	1
9	3	7	8	6	1	4	2	5
8	2	6	7	5	9	3	1	4
7	1	5	6	4	8	2	9	3
6	9	4	5	3	7	1	8	2
1	4	8	9	7	2	5	3	6

10/

9	3	6	1	4	7	2	8	5
3	6	9	4	7	1	5	2	8
6	9	3	7	1	4	8	5	2
8	2	5	9	3	6	1	7	4
5	8	2	6	9	3	7	4	1
2	5	8	3	6	9	4	1	7
1	4	7	2	5	8	3	9	6
7	1	4	8	2	5	9	6	3
4	7	1	5	8	2	6	3	9

The Young Samurai

WOLVES & SHEEP SLITHERLINK

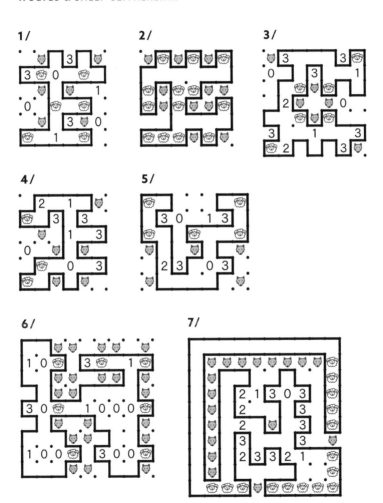

8/

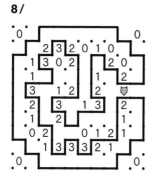

9/

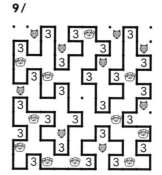

10/

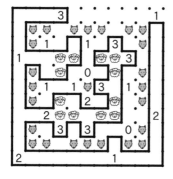

SKYSCRAPERS

1/

```
          2
3 | 1  2  4  3 |
  | 4  3  1  2 | 3
  | 3  4  2  1 |
  | 2  1  3  4 |
    3  2  2
```

2/

```
2 | 4  1  2  3  5 |
  | 3  5  1  2  4 |
  | 2  4  5  1  3 | 2
  | 1  3  4  5  2 | 2
  | 5  2  3  4  1 | 3
        4        5
```

3/

```
    2     3     3
  | 4  1  2  5  3 |
  | 5  3  1  2  4 | 2
3 | 3  2  4  1  5 |
  | 2  5  3  4  1 | 3
  | 1  4  5  3  2 |
    4     1     2
```

4/

```
          4
2 | 4  3  1  5  2 | 2
  | 5  4  2  3  1 |
2 | 1  5  3  2  4 | 2
  | 2  1  5  4  3 |
3 | 3  2  4  1  5 | 1
          2
```

5/

```
       2  2
  | 5  4  3  2  1 |
2 | 3  5  2  1  4 |
2 | 4  3  1  5  2 |
  | 1  2  5  4  3 | 3
  | 2  1  4  3  5 |
          4
```

SUM SKYSCRAPERS

1/

```
  5 6 7 8 9
 ┌─┬─┬─┬─┬─┐
 │5│1│2│3│4│
 ├─┼─┼─┼─┼─┤
 │4│5│1│2│3│
 ├─┼─┼─┼─┼─┤
 │3│4│5│1│2│
 ├─┼─┼─┼─┼─┤
 │2│3│4│5│1│
 ├─┼─┼─┼─┼─┤
 │1│2│3│4│5│
 └─┴─┴─┴─┴─┘
```

2/

```
   8       13
  ┌─┬─┬─┬─┬─┐
  │3│5│4│1│2│
  ├─┼─┼─┼─┼─┤
  │5│4│2│3│1│ 13
  ├─┼─┼─┼─┼─┤
  │1│3│5│2│4│
  ├─┼─┼─┼─┼─┤
14│2│1│3│4│5│
  ├─┼─┼─┼─┼─┤
  │4│2│1│5│3│
  └─┴─┴─┴─┴─┘
   14      8
```

3/

```
   5       6
  ┌─┬─┬─┬─┬─┐
  │5│4│3│1│2│
  ├─┼─┼─┼─┼─┤
 9│1│3│2│5│4│
  ├─┼─┼─┼─┼─┤
  │2│5│4│3│1│
  ├─┼─┼─┼─┼─┤
  │4│1│5│2│3│ 8
  ├─┼─┼─┼─┼─┤
  │3│2│1│4│5│
  └─┴─┴─┴─┴─┘
      7     5
```

4/

```
       20 15
   ┌─┬─┬─┬─┬─┬─┐
   │5│6│1│2│4│3│
   ├─┼─┼─┼─┼─┼─┤
 20│2│3│4│1│5│6│
   ├─┼─┼─┼─┼─┼─┤
 15│4│5│2│3│6│1│
   ├─┼─┼─┼─┼─┼─┤
   │6│1│5│4│3│2│ 20
   ├─┼─┼─┼─┼─┼─┤
   │3│2│6│5│1│4│ 15
   ├─┼─┼─┼─┼─┼─┤
   │1│4│3│6│2│5│
   └─┴─┴─┴─┴─┴─┘
        9 6
```

5/

```
        20 18 17
   ┌─┬─┬─┬─┬─┬─┐
   │5│4│6│2│3│1│
   ├─┼─┼─┼─┼─┼─┤
   │6│5│1│3│4│2│
   ├─┼─┼─┼─┼─┼─┤
   │2│6│4│1│5│3│
   ├─┼─┼─┼─┼─┼─┤
 14│1│3│2│4│6│5│
   ├─┼─┼─┼─┼─┼─┤
   │4│2│3│5│1│6│
   ├─┼─┼─┼─┼─┼─┤
   │3│1│5│6│2│4│
   └─┴─┴─┴─┴─┴─┘
    13 12 11
```

EDAMAME

1/

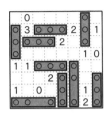

2/

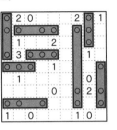

3/

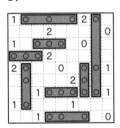

4/

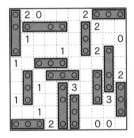

5/

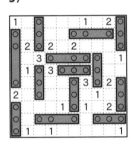

6/

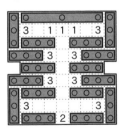

SLASH PACK

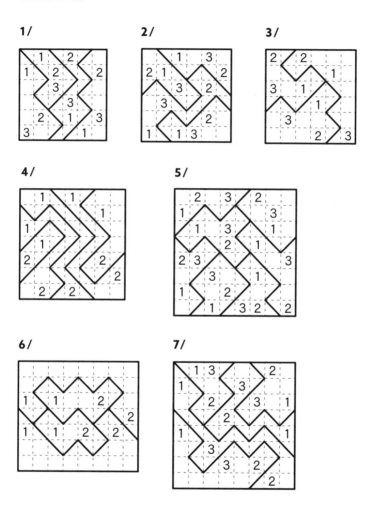

8 /

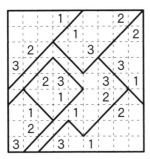

9 /

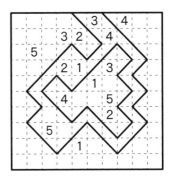

10 /

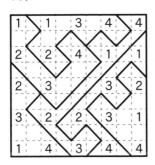

CURVE DATA

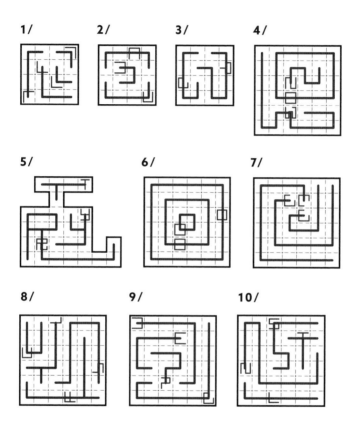